Marching To Different Drummers

Pat Burke Guild and Stephen Garger

Copyright 1985 by Pat Burke Guild and Stephen Garger.
Printed in the United States of America.

Composition by Scott Photographics, Inc.
Printing by Jarboe Printing Company, 1985, 1988, 1991.

ASCD publications present a variety of viewpoints. The views expressed or implied
in this book are not necessarily official positions of the Association.

Price: $7.50
ASCD Stock Number: 611-85410
ISBN: 0-87120-133-X
Library of Congress
  Card Catalog No.: 85-72942

CONTENTS

Foreword

DURING THE PAST DECADE EDUCATORS HAVE BECOME INCREASINGLY AWARE THAT individual learners approach academic tasks with different styles. We have come to recognize that varying styles can mean that some students, teachers, and administrators will be far more successful than others with particular tasks, situations, and people.

Articles and workshops on learning, teaching, and leadership styles have often left the impression that emphasis on learning style, for example, is a complex way to individualize. Educators who have experience with other approaches to individualization may have dismissed learning styles as impractical. While individualization may be perceived as a "nice thing to do," limited resources and emerging evidence on the importance of direct instruction in effective schools have led many schools to move away from the individualized learning programs that gained popularity in the 1970s.

Attention to learning styles is more than a way of individualizing. While based in recognition of individual differences, a focus on learning styles can be a significant step for promoting *equity* in schools. For instance, if the visual learner has less opportunity to learn than the auditory learner because of prevalent teaching behaviors, not only has that learner been shortchanged, but our society has been deprived of the optimum talents of that individual. The mission of ASCD is to "develop leadership for quality in education for ALL students." As we learn to open classroom opportunities to individuals with different learning styles, we will be better able to provide equity, making sure that ALL students gain at least the essential knowledge, skills, and attitudes necessary for success.

Marching to Different Drummers provides an opportunity for us as educators to become familiar with a wide variety of approaches to style. As we read it, we may even find an approach to individual differences that matches our own style of teaching or administration. Our challenge is to read to the rhythm of a drum beat that constantly asks the question, "How can knowing this about style help me to open educational opportunities to students who need it most?"

CAROLYN S. HUGHES
ASCD President, 1985-86

Introduction

If a man does not keep pace with his companions, perhaps it is because he hears a different drummer. Let him step to the music which he hears, however measured or far away.

—Henry David Thoreau

DO YOU SEARCH FOR A FIVE-CENT ERROR IN YOUR CHECKBOOK? WHY?

Some people say they enjoy the challenge of balancing their checkbooks exactly. Some people feel the job isn't done until the exact balance is figured. And some people want to find the nickel before the error escalates.

Then there are those who have forgotten the last time they balanced a checkbook—or even looked at the balance statement from the bank. They wonder why anyone would waste time searching for such a small error. They know that keeping a checkbook is necessary, but they won't spend any more time with it than required.

And, of course, there are many people who are in between these extremes—they search for a $5 error but write off the nickel.

Why do people vary in their approaches to this task? Why do some people say that "you're supposed to," or "it's the right thing to do," while others deride it as "compulsiveness" and "perfectionism?" Do we learn these behaviors from our parents? Maybe, but how do we explain that siblings often handle their checkbooks very differently?

Why would someone handle the checkbook for an organization with care and accuracy, yet be casual about a personal account? And why does the "math whiz" not balance his personal checkbook when obviously it's an easy task?

A natural response to all these questions is that people are different—fundamentally different in what they care about and what they will spend time on. This is simply basic common sense, but it has tremendous implications for educators.

Individual Differences in Education

Individual differences have intrigued and challenged educators for centuries. On the one hand, our profession is motivated by the understanding and application of this concept. On the other hand, practical response to individual differences has almost entirely eluded us. Nathaniel Cantor (1946) is one educator who acknowledges, "that there are individual differences in learning has been recognized in theory as often as it has been denied in practice." (p. 185).

This book is based on the belief that people are different. It describes a variety of ways people differ in personality traits and defines them as differences in style.

The stylistic differences addressed in this book have been variously labeled as learning style, cognitive style, teaching style, leadership style, and psychological type. While the names differ, many of the basic concepts are similar, and we have chosen to address them as related topics.

Does balancing a checkbook affect people in education? Perhaps not directly, but if the reason for handling the checkbook in a certain way reveals a basic aspect of personality, then that trait will somehow be reflected in learning, teaching, or administration. There *is* an important difference, for example, when one teacher thinks that a creative-writing assignment should be neat, detailed, and spelled correctly, while another teacher values a free flow of ideas in which errors can be corrected later. It *does* matter that teachers understand that a "perfect paper" is fundamentally important to some students, but "getting the job done" is good enough for others. It is important to know if an administrator expects a teacher to complete the text and bases part of an evaluation on that criterion. When some parents believe that schools should prepare students for the "real world" of jobs and earning a living and other parents want schools to provide a "liberal arts" education, their basic differences will be reflected in a variety of ways, such as a vote on a music-and- art-program budget. These are only a few examples of how personal individual differences are reflected in all aspects of education.

Our experiences in studying and applying research on styles, teaching about styles, and listening to students and fellow educators talk about styles lead us to believe that style is the most important concept to demand attention in education in many years. Style is at the core of what it means to be a person. It is an old concept that has been explored for centuries, but recently infused with new energy and direction. It is essential to any educator's philosophy of education, and consequently it affects how we view our educational system. It touches on classroom practice, administration, and curriculum development. It relates to staff development and to students' study habits. It helps us to understand ourselves and trust that all students can learn. Perhaps most importantly, it calls upon educators to recognize actively that people are different, and these differences inevitably surface when people learn, teach, supervise, and develop programs.

"Differences in our schools will always exist because teachers and students are people, and a fundamental characteristic of people is diversity," one principal wrote. Then, having acknowledged this fact, he decided to view it positively: "I have often found it possible to transform differences among children, teachers, parents, and administrators into powerful educational assets" (Barth, 1980, 15 and xvii).

Fundamental personality differences do have the potential to bring diverse talents to educational concerns. But if the differences are treated superficially—"You could see it my way if you only wanted to!"—we will certainly miss the opportunities of diverse energy and continue to deny the differences in the everyday practices of schools.

The Purpose of This Book

This book explores differences in style to help educators fulfill their responsibilities and experience the joys of helping people realize their full potential.

Fortunately, there is a wealth of research on differences in style, but summaries of these theories and ideas are not easily assessable. In response, this book describes major research contributions and identifies common themes. It presents a summary of concepts but consciously does not strive to create one synergistic definition from the different approaches to style.

For those relatively new to the theory of style, there are basic definitions and examples. For those generally familiar with it, the summary of different theories, the identification of basic themes, and the wide range of suggestions for application should provide food for thought. And to those very knowledgeable about research on styles, we offer our reflections and personal experiences.

This book is intended for all practicing educators. Teachers will recognize its messages about themselves and their students and will benefit from the practical classroom suggestions. Administrators should find the information relevant to all aspects of their jobs and the suggestions immediately applicable to their work as instructional leaders. Curriculum specialists should be able to use the philosophical framework as well as the direct suggestions. University and college instructors should find the synthesis of complex concepts useful for introducing style to their students. Parents can take personal meaning from the book by "seeing" themselves and their children in the descriptions and gaining support from the message to celebrate diversity.

Our approach is comprehensive, but we do not attempt to cover the entire field. This book provides theory to enable informed and wise use of the concepts. It offers practical suggestions while urging readers to decide thoughtfully which applications best suit their situations.

The concept of style is both complex and simple. Each view is partially true and each can be dangerous alone. An oversimplified view can lead to naive action; yet a complex view can result in no action at all. We believe that the message of diversity of style is timely and important—and in this book we invite you to join with us to find ways for our schools to give all students the opportunity to fulfill their potential.

Our Perspectives and Personal Bias

We have studied and observed style in a number of different situations. We know about style from our experiences as teachers and administrators. We balance that experience with academic research on style. And perhaps most importantly, we continue to learn about style by sharing the concepts with other administrators, teachers, and parents. Working with thousands of thoughtful and talented educators has strengthened our resolve about the importance of style and deepened our understanding of the concepts.

Our practical experience and academic reflection lead us to bring certain perspectives to these theories. And, of course, our individual styles are reflected in this book. You should know some of our biases.

First, individual human differences are positive—and should be a resource to schools. We agree with Tomlinson, who wrote that "effective schooling should expand the differences between students rather than restrict them" (in Mackenzie, 1983, p. 13). When students learn and grow in their own way, differences are pronounced. When we decide we want to value differences, we will make decisions that expand diversity rather than seek uniformity and inappropriate conformity.

Second, active recognition of individual differences challenges any "best" answer for an educational question. We have to ask "best for whom, in what situation, and under what circumstances?" In their description of the school improvement processes, Bruce Joyce and his colleagues make clear early on that "there simply is no best model for a school.... There are many effective models for schooling, but they do not work equally well for all children, nor do they achieve all purposes to the same degree" (1983, p. 9). Nor can any one program or instructional strategy be "best" for every student.

Third, we believe that differences in style are more than variations in behavior. When I act differently than you, it is because my behavior makes sense to me. Behavior "makes sense" because it is an external reflection of how I understand a situation. Thus the study of style must explore differences in behavior and recognize the roots of the behavior. This also implies that fundamental characteristics of style will be reflected in various aspects of behavior—in learning, teaching, administration, and personality in general. These areas must be studied together, or we run the risk of shallow applications. For example, we would want to avoid "doing" learning styles for students while treating all the staff the same.

Fourth, the variety of perspectives on style and diverse models proposed by researchers offers a rich source of theories, experiences and suggestions for educational applications. We should draw from various theories to the extent that they can offer suggestions for our particular situations. In this book we do not advocate any single model but urge the reader to study thoughtfully, examine the perspective and bias of the researchers, form a personal approach to style, and select appropriate ideas for application.

Fifth, we believe in the importance of the individual teacher's decisions in the classroom. In his review of effective school research Mackenzie (1983) says, "No strategy works in isolation from the teacher's judgment and discrimination" (p. 10). Thus knowledge of styles should provide guidance for wise judgments. This book is not designed as a cookbook but rather as a source book for the hundreds of decisions educators are challenged with each day.

Sixth and finally, we are enthusiastic about the power provided by knowledge of styles, but we also recognize this knowledge is not a panacea for problems in schools. Knowing about differences in style will not make good educators out of cynical, incompetent teachers or administrators. Knowledge of styles will not guarantee effectiveness or excellence in schools. But it does point us in the direction of using the unique talents of both adults and children to make our schools better for all.

User's Guide

The book is in three parts. The first part defines style and provides some background into research on it. The second part describes six different style applications. The final section presents a way to organize your thinking about styles, raises additional issues, and discusses implementation and staff development. A comprehensive annotated bibliography is provided to aid the reader in further study.

The book reviews the work of six major researchers and provides an example of application for each research model. The six were chosen to represent major efforts historically and conceptually. Carl Jung's work is comprehensive and has developed through nearly a century of examination. Psychologist Herman A. Witkin's work is the most extensive and in-depth research on cognitive style conducted in the past 50 years. The modality information, represented here by Walter Barbe and Raymond Swassing and by Rita and Kenneth Dunn, has consistently intrigued educators. And the work of the Dunns, Anthony Gregorc, and Bernice McCarthy has brought these concepts directly to teachers. In this book we can only touch upon the work of these researchers. We urge you to study the original sources listed in the annotated bibliography for a fuller understanding of each model.

We invite and encourage you to approach the book with your own style: browse, skip around, read and reflect. We have also attempted to address the different ways you can know about style by including personal examples, research findings, practical applications, and philosophical implications. We hope that as you read you will discover new questions about style.

Some of the book is factual—it reports information—and some is interpretive—it synthesizes our experiences and beliefs. Many of the ideas will provoke questions. The more one studies individual differences, the more complexities one finds. This fact alone reinforces our belief in the importance of the concepts and the need for further exploration.

Some ideas are so simple that experienced educators will recognize them immediately. But acting on the concepts is never simple; practicing personalized education is a challenge for even the most experienced among us. We need both the inspiration of theory and the wisdom of experience to guide us.

And so, as always, teachers and administrators are called upon to bring to bear the talents and skills that make them good at their jobs—especially the ability to keep their "heads in the clouds" while their "feet are planted firmly on the ground" (Guild, 1982, p.6).

PART I

DEFINING STYLES

1. Style: What and Why

A fact is not what is; a fact for any person is what he believes is so.

—Arthur Combs
Helping Relationships

SOME PEOPLE WE KNOW HAVE A STYLE OF DRESS. SOME HAVE A DISTINCT STYLE OF speech, perhaps an indication of regional roots. Some athletes bring their own styles to their sports.

When we use "style" in these ways, we are saying that there is a recognizable pattern in a person's dress, speech, or sport. As an "outsider," I see this pattern, associate it with the person, and find it typical and relatively consistent. Certainly a person does not always dress, speak, or play in the same way, but a person's usual behavior is predictable enough.

The way each of us perceives the world governs how we think, make judgments, and form values about experiences and people. Our personal perspective is our window on the world. This unique aspect of our humanness is what we call style. It is based on the fact that, as Carl Jung (1921) observed, "besides the many individual differences in human psychology there are also typical differences" (p. 3).

How about you? Do you notice immediately when a friend or colleague gets a new pair of glasses or changes hairstyle? Have you ever described a car accident only to find out that another witness reported the same event quite differently? How do you view an abstract painting? Do you try to figure out what it is? Or do you react to the mood or colors? Differences in perception help explain why people *see* things differently even though everyone may be physically capable of seeing the same things.

What's your morning routine? Do you have a daily set pattern for dressing, showering, having breakfast? Does it bother you when the pattern is disturbed or would such a rigid routine bore you? Those of us who behave in an orderly, systematic, linear way probably form our ideas and think that way, too. Your daily behavior patterns often reflect your thinking processes.

Are you a Rubik's Cube fan? Are you intrigued by the challenge of such a puzzle or do you find it a waste of time? Do you know how many countries are on the continent of Africa? Are you interested? Do you want to know the practical purpose of a task before you are willing to give it your effort?

Do you make decisions with your heart or your head? Do you buy a new car by carefully weighing data from automotive reports, or do you simply buy the model and color you've always wanted? When you disagree with someone, do you worry how he or she will take your comments? Just as differences in what motivates and interests each of us reflect our unique perspectives, so do a person's criteria for decisions and judgments reflect one's style.

These basic patterns in personality influence many aspects of personal and professional behavior. In general they are called personality styles. When they affect learning, we refer to learning styles. When the patterns are reflected in teaching, we call them teaching styles. And our particular management patterns are called leadership or administrative styles.

About Style

When people are introduced to the concept of style, they often say, "You mean there are other people like me!" It's a comment said half in jest, but often with a serious note. "I really am OK!" usually follows, and lots of questions emerge as a person thinks about style. Some of the typical comments and questions have led us to identify a few general assumptions about style that are explored further throughout the book:

1. "Yes, Virginia, everyone has style!" Each person is unique and complex, and yet each person is predictable, too. It's the predictable side of people that announces their style. The "way I am," the "that's just me" parts of each of us are our patterns—our style. These patterns give us familiar ways to approach life and provide stability, maturity, and psychological health. They give us some things in common with other people, but their particular combination and intensity make each of us unique. As you study words that describe style, it will be helpful to think about your own "style profile."

2. "I'm OK, you're OK!" style is basically neutral. While I may not like someone's pattern of speech, for example, I realize that it is natural for that person and probably for his or her family, friends, and neighbors. Certainly some people do have speech disabilities, but their style does not directly indicate a problem.

3. "Still waters run deep!" style is basically stable, but behaviors emanating from it may change according to the situation. If I'm a detail-oriented person, exacting and perfectionistic, this trait has probably been with me from childhood and will remain with me throughout life. But the behaviors that reflect this trait will most likely adapt to the situation. At the office my files may be carefully organized, but at home I'm probably resigned to a more flexible organization of the refrigerator, which the whole family uses.

4. "Yes, but!" style is not absolute. Just as a staunch Republican may vote for a certain Democratic candidate, so too there will be specific exceptions to pervasive style patterns. I may typically make decisions in an objective, cool-headed way except when they relate to money, for example. However, if my behavior regularly fluctuates in a certain aspect of my life, it is possible that either I don't have a defined pattern or that contrasting patterns are pulling at me in different directions.

5. "I could if I wanted to!" style alone does not determine competence. I may not balance my checkbook, but I am able to if I decide it's necessary or my job requires it. I may not notice your new hairstyle, but if you point it out, I'm certainly capable of seeing it. At some point, our style does make certain tasks easier or harder and thus is related to a person's strengths and weaknesses. But we can become reasonably competent at many things by approaching them with our own style.

6. "It takes one to know one!" style traits are easier to recognize in others if I personally understand those characteristics. People who know a New York accent, for example, immediately recognize that speech pattern. If I hear a practical question; I tune in if I, too, value practicality. If I simply don't understand someone, it's likely that our styles are very different.

These assumptions and examples help us to see the simple and complex nature of style. While many things are known about style, there is also much to be discovered and explained. As you read further expect a confirmation of the depth of the style theory. It is a theory that seeks to help us understand basic human nature.

Style in Education

Education is a people business. Perhaps every issue, decision, and problem that we deal with in schools is basically a human relations situation. The effectiveness of curriculum, instruction, discipline, management, community relationships, and the degree of academic achievement can often be traced to the ability of people to identify common purposes and work productively together. Where we find open communication, high morale, positive climate, commitment of community and parents, and enthusiastic, caring professionals, we find excellence in learning and teaching.

If education is a people business, and if we know that people are different, then education is a business about the diversity of people. It is about the different goals people have for education. It is about the different programs people want in schools. It is about the multitude of values and interests of all its constituents.

Yet even as we verbally accept the existence of diversity, we also recognize how often it is ignored in practice. We make rules for a school assuming that everyone values and interprets them in the same way. We talk with staff and students and assume that our intentions are communicated as clearly as our actual words. We search for the right or best programs and methods for helping all students to learn.

Here's where the study of style is particularly important. Knowing that people see different things helps us to communicate with more depth. Knowing that people have different beliefs and values helps us to understand the various interests and needs of a diverse school population. Accepting the diversity of style can help us to create the atmosphere and experiences that encourage each individual to reach his or her full potential.

A Variety of Differences

In what ways are people different?

What general things are we talking about when we say people are different?

Perhaps the most comprehensive statement we can make is that people have different personalities. Yes, but what is personality, and how are people different? We can see, of course, that people act differently. However, to understand different behaviors we need to look into the roots of people's actions.

One way to do this is to recognize several basic functions that we all perform when interacting with a situation, a person, information, or ideas. First we take in the situation, then we think about it, react to it, and ultimately act upon it. These basic functions guided us to create four categories of style differences:

- Style is concerned with cognition: people perceive and gain knowledge differently.
- Style is concerned with conceptualization: people form ideas and think differently.
- Style is concerned with affect: people feel and form values differently.
- Style is concerned with behavior: people act differently.

These categories are proposed to help organize the diverse aspects of style but are not meant to be rigid. The complexity and subtlety of human behavior make any organization of individual differences accurate in one instance but then arbitrary in the next. To understand styles and their implications for education, it will be helpful to think about these categories while always keeping in mind that all the characteristics are integrated in the total personality of a real human being.

Cognition: "How Do I Know?"

Perception, the initial stage of cognition, involves receiving, taking possession of, obtaining, and discerning information, ideas, and concepts. Some of us perceive best what is real, while others clearly see possibilities with their imaginations. Some people see parts of a whole, separating ideas from their context, while others see the whole—not unlike the difference between seeing the trees or the forest.

These perceptual differences affect what is received and how it is received. My best intentions and the most extensive efforts to convince another to see exactly as I see will not eliminate these personal differences. A gifted artist can describe the gestalt of a painting, but some viewer will be struck by, and confined to, an image of an exaggerated cow's head, for example. The artist can plead, cajole, and discuss the work in detail, but to little avail if the viewer's perception governs a certain view. You may take a hike through the woods with a friend who suddenly becomes fascinated with a mushroom. At first you actually may not even see the mushroom—your friend needs to point it out. Then, even when you physically see it, it doesn't mean the same thing to you. Your perceptions are different.

Two people listening to the same music will respond differently to the nuances of the sound, reflecting the depth of their musical experiences as well as their personal perceptions. Perhaps one is tuned to certain subtleties, while the other is a more general listener. Two people sit next to each other at a movie and are surprised that they recall different things when they discuss the film later. Children in a class often hear directions in very different ways.

Gaining knowledge is another part of cognition; people get information in different ways. Some people use abstract sources, reading about things and listening to others' descriptions; others need concrete experiences. The concrete[1] person will often depend directly on the senses for information: "I see it; now I know what it is." The abstract person is more receptive to secondhand sources of knowledge. Some people have to touch something or see it operate before they accept it as real, while others can imagine a vivid reality without needing to experience it. There are also sensory specialists—those people who rely on one sense more than another to gather information. Again, these different ways of getting information and gaining knowledge are reflective of distinct personal styles.

Conceptualization: "How Do I Think?"

People also exhibit differences in what they do with the knowledge they gain—how they process information and how they think. Some people are most typically convergers, always looking for connections, ways to tie things together. Others are more divergent—one thought, idea, or fact triggers a multitude of new directions. Some people order ideas, information, and experiences in a very linear, sequential way, while others organize their thoughts in clusters and random patterns. Some people think aloud. They verbalize ideas as a way of understanding them. Others concentrate on understanding concepts and experiences privately in their own minds. Some people think quickly, spontaneously, and impulsively; others are slower and more reflective.

We see these examples, and others, everyday. You may have had the experience of saying to someone, "Whatever made you say that?" and then realizing the person was thinking about something in a very different way than you were. The important point is that people naturally perceive, gain

---

[1]It is important to distinguish between styles and developmental stages. Those who research style do not address themselves directly to the concrete stage of acquiring knowledge, but rather say that at any age, whatever the developmental state, some people are more or less concrete in their style, relative to their appropriate stage of development.

knowledge, and process in different ways. These differences form patterns for each person and affect a person's total behavior.

Affect: "How Do I Decide?"

Differences in motivation, judgments, values, and emotional responses also characterize individual style. Some people are motivated internally; others seek external rewards. Some people actively seek to please others—children to please their parents and teachers, adults to please bosses and spouses—while some people are not attuned to others' expectations, and still others will rebel against such demands. Some people make decisions logically, rationally, objectively, and with cool heads. Others often decide things subjectively, focusing on perceptions and emotions—their own and others.' Some people seek frequent feedback on their ideas and work, some are crushed by slight criticism, others welcome analytical comments, and still others don't even ask an outsider for a critique.

For some people the medium is the message, while others focus directly on the content. Some people are emotionally involved in everything they do, and others are characteristically neutral. The emotional learner prefers a classroom with a high emotional charge while another kind of learner works best in a low-key environment. These affective differences are also stylistic and interrelated with the conceptual and cognitive characteristics discussed above.

The discussion of differences in affective style does not contradict basic humanistic beliefs in education. Everyone does best in a supportive atmosphere free from excessive criticism. An awareness of stylistic differences can help administrators and teachers to recognize that every person does not seek the same affective response and to understand the kinds of support various people want.

Behavior: "How Do I Act?"

Cognitive, conceptual, and affective patterns are the roots of behavior, and pervasive and consistent stylistic characteristics will be reflected in a person's actions.

The reflective thinker, for example, can be expected to act in a reflective way in a variety of behavioral situations from decision making to relating to people. Some people scan a situation to get the gist before tackling a problem; others focus on a certain part of the problem immediately and start

Figure 1. Some Examples of Style Characteristics

Category	Characteristics*	Researchers
COGNITION perceiving, finding out, getting information	sensing/intuition	Jung, Myers-Briggs, Mok, Keirsey and Bates
	field dependent/field independent	Witkin
	abstract/concrete	Gregorc, Kolb and McCarthy
	visual, auditory, kinesthetic, tactile	Barbe and Swassing, Dunn and Dunn
CONCEPTUALIZATION thinking, forming ideas, processing, memory	extravert/introvert	Jung, Myers-Briggs, Keirsey and Bates
	reflective observation/ active experimentation	Kolb and McCarthy
	random/sequential	Gregorc
AFFECT feelings, emotional response, motivation, values, judgments	feeler/thinker	Jung, Myers-Briggs, Mok, Keirsey and Bates
	effect of temperature, light, food, time of day, sound, design	Dunn and Dunn

BEHAVIOR

manifestations of all of the above-mentioned characteristics

*Characteristics separated by a slash (/) indicate bipolar or opposite traits.

with it. Some people approach a task randomly; others are very systematic. Some people need explicit structure; others prefer and perform best in a more open-ended situation. Some people prefer to work alone, others with groups, and some prefer working in certain physical environments.

In education we recognize a variety of differences in how people learn—how these basic styles affect the individual learner's behavior. Reflective students are slow to respond to questions and need to think a response through carefully; impulsive learners make a quick response and blurt out their thoughts. The step-by-step person learns only when each step is clear and the transitions are spelled out. Another kind of learner typically makes intuitive leaps. After several weeks of struggling with division of fractions, this student may suddenly announce, "I've got it!" This same intuitive learner will also often be impatient with sounding out parts of a word and doing phonetic worksheets when she has already grasped the essence of a story.

In sum, people have differences in the ways they perceive, think, process knowledge, feel, and behave. Many specific examples of these differences have been identified by researchers (see Figure 1) and are discussed in the next chapters. Equally important, the personal and professional experiences of educators provide constant evidence that these style differences do exist and that they affect many aspects of the learning-teaching process.

2. A Brief History of Style

For as in one body we have many members, and all the members do not have the same function, so we, though many, are one body in Christ, and individually members one of another. Having gifts that differ according to the grace given to us, let us use them.
— Romans 12:4-6a

Let A be some experience from which a number of thinkers start. Let Z be the practical conclusion rationally inferrible from it. One gets to the conclusion by one line, another by another; one follows a course of English, another of German, verbal imagery. With one, visual images predominate; with another, tactile. Some trains are tinged with emotions, others not; some are very abridged, synthetic and rapid, others, hesitating and broken into many steps. But when the penultimate terms of all the trains, however differing inter se, finally shoot into the same conclusion, we say, and rightly say, that all the thinkers have had substantially the same thought. It would probably astound each of them beyond measure to be let into his neighbor's mind and to find how different the scenery there was from that in his own.

THE EMINENT AMERICAN PSYCHOLOGIST, PHILOSOPHER, AND EDUCATOR WILLIAM James wrote the above words in *The Principles of Psychology* in 1890, illustrating that style as a distinctive and characteristic trait has long been a concern of psychologists and educators as they seek to describe the many facets of an individual.

It is not clear who first actually used the term style in this way. The Greek physician Hippocrates identified Sanguine, Choleric, Melancholy, and Phlegmatic personalities. For most of this century, the research has been conducted primarily in the field of psychology. German psychologists were exploring individual cognitive style differences at the turn of the century. Perhaps best known among them is Carl Jung, whose research into "psychological types" first appeared in 1921.

The word style is used in American psychologist Gordon W. Allport's work in the 1930s as he defines consistent patterns appearing in individuals. Allport (1961) notes that interest in individual differences in psychology "grew up at the beginning of this century" and that "many psychologists would consider this movement as coextensive with the psychology of personality" (p. 15). Many of these personality theories are based upon studies that were conducted regarding perception:

> Perception is *the* point of reality contact, the door to reality appraisal, and there is no doubt that here especially are the selective, adaptive controls of personality brought into play (Klein, 1951:328-329, emphasis in the original).

A look at several experiments carried out at this time will provide some examples to illustrate the importance that psychologist Klein placed on perception as "the point of reality contact."

In 1945 Lowenfeld reported a distinction between visual and haptic types, with the former experiencing the world primarily through vision and the latter primarily through touch. In his tests he discovered that one person in four depends upon touch and kinesthesis rather than upon vision.

In work he did during the late 1940s and early 1950s, Klein (1951) found that "a person continually brings to bear in any kind of situation what for him are 'preferred' ways of meeting reality" (p. 336). Whereas Lowenfeld spoke of preferences in terms of visual and haptic types, Klein speaks of levelers and sharpeners:

> [the] leveling group followed a pattern which we called "self- inwardness" and emphasized a retreat from objects, avoidance of competition or of any situation requiring active manipulation. [The sharpening group] defines people who generally find competition and exhibitionism congenial, who have high needs for attainment, who energetically and oftentimes aggressively push themselves forward, and who have a great need for autonomy (p. 336).

Herman A. Witkin began his work on perception in the late 1940s and continued it until his death in 1979. Witkin proposed the existence of different perceptual tendencies in persons depending on how they view and use their surroundings. He spoke of people as being field dependent or field independent. In tests designed to determine reliance on cues received from the background field if

the performance range perception is strongly dominated by the prevailing field, that mode of perception was designated "field dependent." At the other extreme, where the person experiences items as more or less separate from the surrounding field, the designation "field independent" was used (Witkin et. al., 1977:7).

Allport (1961) defines cognitive style as "distinctive ways of living in the world" (p. 271). Prior to 1955 psychologists had identified several classifications of people that served to illustrate Allport's "distinctiveness"—including the designations visual/haptic; levelers/sharpeners; field dependent/field independent, all discussed above.

Unfortunately, research into individual differences gradually diminished. Leona Tyler (1965) attributes this decline to the fact that since

tests of this sort showed very little relationship to school success, the enthusiasm of psychologists for the whole mental-test movement was considerably dampened. Because tests of the kind that Binet and Henri had been recommending, tapping complex intellectual characteristics rather than perceptual sensitivities, stood up better under this kind of evaluation, they set the pattern for later work, and the attempt to measure perceptual differences was largely abandoned (p. 212).

In other words, school success (measured in terms of good grades) could be proven to relate to a student's IQ. A high IQ indicated the potential for a high grade. On the other hand, in overall terms, a field-dependent student did not do better or worse in school than a field-independent student. Whereas it was "better" to have a high IQ rather than a low IQ, it could not be proven that it was better to have a certain perceptual sensitivity. In terms of school success, style by itself was neutral.

In addition to the diminishing interest on the part of research psychologists in the topic, there was little or no communication between education and psychology regarding individual differences. Educators were either not aware of the cognitive style research or ignored it

partly because many of the studies were conducted in fields other than education, and partly because educators. . . have emphasized *programs* rather than *individual* learning styles (Dunn and Dunn, 1975b:44, emphasis in the original).

Therefore in both education and psychology the possibility that the world might actually look, sound, and feel differently to different persons, that they might solve problems and form concepts in quite different ways, and that the same stimulating situation might carry different meanings for them was something investigators did not generally take into account (Tyler, 1965:211).

Style in Education

Since the late 1960s educators have been directly addressing the "possibility" cited above by Tyler. Anthony Gregorc (1982) speaks of different mind qualities, describing how we take in and how we process information. Rita and Kenneth Dunn (1975a) have investigated a number of learning preferences, which they organize by categories of four stimuli. Several applications of Carl Jung's original identification of psychological types have been made for education, and the identification of modality sensitivities has been studied by a number of educators.

Educators are now regularly drawing on the fields of psychology and neurobiology in order to expand their awareness of individual differences. Studies of brain functioning and its relationship to learning are intriguing teachers and administrators and stimulating broader approaches to curriculum and methods of instruction. The recent work of Howard Gardner (1983) expands the way we think about intelligence by identifying multiple intelligences, including musical intelligence, bodily-kinesthetic intelligence, and personal intelligence. Interest in the potential of the human mind is bringing fascinating theories and challenges to schools.

Through these various approaches, education is now actively engaged in understanding and recognizing individual differences. This movement is profound and important. In his introduction to a collection of papers on research in style and brain behavior, James Keefe (1982) says

> Knowledge about learning styles and brain behavior is a fundamental new tool at the service of teachers and schools. It is clearly not the latest educational fad. It provides a deeper and more profound view of the learner than previously perceived, and is part of a basic framework upon which a sounder theory and practice of learning and instruction may be built.

This current focus builds upon a solid foundation of theory and practice in both psychology and education. It should have pervasive and long-lasting effects.

PART II

EXAMPLES
OF STYLE

Figure 2. Examples of Applications of Style and Models of Research

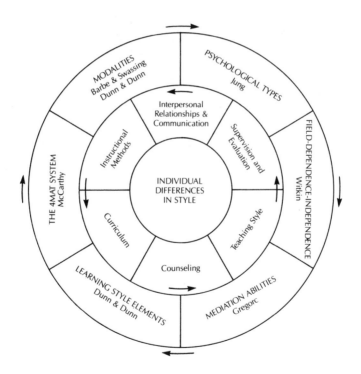

The next six chapters illustrate several areas in education that are affected by individual differences in style. As each area is discussed, a specific study of style is described. The "match" we have made between a model and an application is intended as only one *example* of use of specific research on style. As the wheel above is rotated, it is clear that each model of style can contribute to each area of implementation.

3. Interpersonal Relationships and Communication
Jung's Psychological Types

"First of all," he said, "if you can learn a simple trick, Scout, you'll get along a lot better with all kinds of folks. You never really understand a person until you consider things from his point of view..."

"Sir?"

"...until you climb into his skin and walk around in it."

—Harper Lee
To Kill a Mockingbird

Mrs. Hand comes to school for the annual parent-teacher conference and asks Mr. Chandler, the teacher, how Darren is doing this year. Mr. Chandler responds, "Darren has completed all of his assignments and regularly hands in his work. He is doing solid work for this grade." Mrs. Hand seems puzzled at this response and comments, "Yes, yes I know, I see his work when he brings it home, but I want to know how he is getting along with the other students."

In the classroom next door, Mrs. Wasson, a parent, asks the teacher, Mrs. Kehle, "How is Jennifer doing this year?" The teacher enthusiastically responds that "Jennifer seems to be getting along with everyone very well." At this point, in frustration, Mrs. Wasson says, "Yes, I know she has friends; she's always gotten along quite well. I want to know about her school-work."

WHEN PARENTS ASK, "HOW'S MY CHILD DOING IN SCHOOL?" WHAT DO THEY MEAN? As Mr. Chandler, Mrs. Kehle, and all teachers know too well, they mean different things. For Mr. Chandler, getting along with other kids may be of secondary importance, but when Darren's mother asks how he is doing, she is asking about interpersonal relationships, not academics. For Mrs. Wasson, her daughter's academics are her primary concern. These different intentions are all too familiar to people who work in schools.

Clear communications and successful interpersonal relationships are the very core of educational decisions and programs. When people get along and understand each other, schools work well. Research into effective schools has labeled it "positive climate," and an extensive study of successful schools in England called it "positive ethos" (Rutter et. al., 1979).

To explore the relationship of style to interpersonal relationships and communication, we will discuss the work of Carl Jung. Other perspectives on style could also be used to illustrate this area, just as Jung's theories affect other issues in education.

Psychological Types—Carl G. Jung

One of the questions that has interested philosophers and psychologists throughout history is why people behave in different ways. Early in this century Carl Jung gave an extensive explanation of behavior patterns in his book, *Psychological Types,* first published in 1921.

Jung proposed that to understand different behaviors we should focus on the basic functions people perform in their lives. He said that every psychologically healthy human being has to operate in a variety of different ways depending on the circumstances, the people, and the situations. But despite situational adaptations, each of us will inevitably tend to develop comfortable patterns that lead us to behave in certain predictable ways. Jung used the word "types" to identify these styles of personality.

One basic function all psychologically healthy human beings have is understanding what is experienced. Jung identified two ways of viewing people and situations. Some people see the world through their senses—vision, hearing, touch, and smell. They observe what is real, what is factual, and what is actually happening. They stick to what they see, and for them seeing is believing. Because of the emphasis on the pragmatic and real, observable aspects of experience and people, Carl Jung called this function *sensation*. This function in each of us enables us to observe carefully, gather facts, and focus on practical actions.

Another way of viewing the world has to do with possibilities and relationships. This way of seeing experiences and people helps us to read between the lines, to attend to meaning, to focus on what is and what might be. This part of our perception helps us to read subtleties, body language, tones of voice, and things that interpret the experiences of the senses. It leads us to look at old problems in creative and original ways. This kind of perception, this way of experiencing the world, Jung called *intuition* because we focus on and react to images our minds create.

Jung explained that everyone uses both kinds of perception when dealing with people and situations, but that we each tend to have a preference for one way of looking at the world. The kind of perception we favor most often becomes our window through which we observe life. Since these ways of looking at the world are fundamentally different, it stands to reason that if we are more likely to search for reality and facts through our senses, we are less likely to depend on and to trust possibilities, imagination, and intuition. Obviously the opposite holds true—intuition leads us to search beneath and beyond reality and to distrust surface information. Our experiences tend to reinforce our way of looking at the world. We are most in tune with people who approach life the way we do and sometimes confused and baffled by people who don't *see* what we see.

Jung also described another fundamental difference among people: individuals approach the decision-making process in different ways. Some of us analyze information, data, situations, and people and apply a logical and rational process to making a decision. We pride ourselves on being objective, calm, cool, and collected. If the decision is difficult, we search for more information. We are slow and careful in our analysis of the data because accuracy and thoroughness are very important. This process of decision-making leads us to trust objectivity, data, logical predictions, and rational arguments. When we arrive at a conclusion, we are confident that all alternatives have been explored and weighed against each other, and that the final decision has been reached unemotionally and carefully. Jung described this function as the *thinking* function.

On the other hand, some of us approach a decision through a subjective, perceptive, empathetic, and emotional perspective. We search for the effect of the decision on ourselves and others. We consider alternatives and examine evidence to develop a personal reaction and commitment. We view the decision-making process as complex and not totally objective. Essentially, we see circumstantial evidence as extremely important. We live in a world of gray rather than black and white and often use the phrase "it depends" to describe the subjective nature of a decision. We will sometimes go against the tide of rational evidence because of some personal perception about a situation or person. This basic human function Jung called the *feeling* function.

Jung explains that every healthy human being uses both thinking and feeling in the decision-making process, but each one of us tends to become more comfortable, and more skilled, in arriving at a decision in either a thinking or feeling way. Again, these functions are opposite on a continuum. Making decisions with an emphasis on logic and reason leads to a distrust of emotions, empathy, and personal perceptions. At the same time a trust in perceptions and personal insight can lead to a casual regard for logic and rational evidence. "Don't confuse me with the facts, my mind's made up" becomes reality.

An important part of Jung's explanation of these four basic human functions was his insistence that no direct value was attached to one's approach to perception or decision making. Accurate, clear, and important perceptions can be gained through both sensation and intuition. Successful, effective, and honest decisions can be made through logical thinking and also through perceptive feelings. A mature approach to life includes a recognition that we need to use both kinds of perception and both kinds of judgment, each for the right purpose. Also we need each other's strengths because

the clearest vision of the future comes only from an intuitive, the most practical realism only from a sensing type, the most incisive analysis only from a thinker, and the most skillful handling of people only from a feeling type. Success for any enterprise demands a variety of types, each in the right place (Myers, 1962:5).

The differences in approach become patterns for us and tend to affect all aspects of our personal and professional behavior. Since people see and think about the world differently, it is not surprising, Jung concluded, that patterns of behavior will be different for people who favor each type.

Another dimension Jung described was the extent to which our behavior is determined by our attitude toward the world. Jung said that many of us operate comfortably and successfully by interacting with things external to us—other people, experiences, situations. Others are most interested in the internal world of their own minds, hearts, and souls. Jung described these differences among people as *extraversion* and *introversion*. Again he said every psychologically healthy human being functions in extraverted ways at times and in introverted ways at other times, but tends to develop patterns that are most typical and most comfortable. Some of us like to test our thoughts and ideas through talking or doing, until they become clearer to us. Others like to mull over our thoughts and our actions, reflecting upon them until they become more valid for us. Those of us who tend toward extraversion often think aloud—or think with our mouths open. Those of us who operate more comfortably in an introverted way are often pensive, reflective, and slow to act because we aren't ready to translate internal thoughts to the external world.

Jung found that the four functions of sensation, intuition, thinking, and feeling will be expressed differently by those with extraverted preferences and those with introverted preferences. An extraverted feeling person would be outwardly emotional and expressive, whereas an introverted feeling person would be reflective and private about emotions, but both would base a final, and successful, decision on the subjective aspects of an issue. Again, Jung was careful to describe the equality of both extraversion and introversion. But he also recognized the problems that may arise when people of opposite kinds of expression communicate and work together.

These four functions and two types of expression provide the basis for Jung's descriptions of human behavior. He believed that we are each born with a tendency toward a particular pattern and that change in human behavior, while possible, is a very slow process. He believed that growth and maturity allow us to develop our own strengths and also to understand other approaches to life.

Applications of Jung's Theory

Carl Jung's theories have been adopted and applied by a variety of researchers throughout this century. When his book was translated into English in the 1920s, Katharine Briggs became interested in the concepts as they applied to her family and the people she knew well. She and her daughter, Isabel Briggs Myers, explored Jung's theories with their family and friends. They became convinced that Jung's work had wide application and tremendous potential for increasing human understanding. Seeing the need for personal understanding of the theories, they developed an instrument that would permit people to learn about their own type. Originally piloted in the 1940s, the Myers-Briggs Type Indicator, the MBTI, has become a well-known and well-respected psychological instrument. Through forced-choice questions and word pairs, people are able to measure their own balance of intuition versus sensation, of thinking versus feeling, and of extraversion versus introversion.

As Briggs and Myers worked with Jung's theories, they became convinced of another important dimension. They believed there is a preference in each individual for the *judging* function or the *perceptive* function. Therefore, they added another continuum to their instrument. The desire to be open-ended and to understand life is labeled "P" for perception, and the desire to bring closure and to regulate life is labeled "J" for judgment. Thus their final instrument includes four continua; the combination of the four continua scores produces 16 different types. (See Figure 3.)

The Myers-Briggs Type Indicator is used extensively by human-resource professionals in industry, by psychologists, by counselors, by those in religious life, and more recently by educators interested in its application to teaching and learning. There are many publications reporting extensive research, some dealing with education. Gordon Lawrence's (1982) book, *People Types and Tiger Stripes, A Practical Guide to Learning Styles,* suggests practical applications for teachers.

Figure 3. Myers-Briggs Dimensions and Types

Extraversion (E) ————————————————————— Introversion (I)

Sensing (S) ————————————————————— Intuition (N)

Thinking (T) ————————————————————— Feeling (F)

Judgment (J) ————————————————————— Perception (P)

ISTJ	ISFJ	INFJ	INTJ
ISTP	ISFP	INFP	INTP
ESTP	ESFP	ENFP	ENTP
ESTJ	ESFJ	ENFJ	ENTJ

In the 1970s psychologists David Keirsey and Marilyn Bates (1978) described their experience with the MBTI in a book called *Please Understand Me, Character and Temperament Types.* They made another adaptation when they simplified the 16 labels into four basic temperaments by clustering the dimensions. They named these temperaments after the Greek gods Apollo (intuition and feeling), Prometheus (intuition and thinking), Epimetheus (sensing and judging), and Dionysus (sensing and perceiving). From Keirsey and Bates' basic temperament descriptions, Keith Golay (1982), an educator, developed applications for the classroom, which are described in his book, *Learning Patterns and Temperament Styles.*

Another application of Jung's work has been made in industry by a management consultant named Paul Mok. Working with the four functions of sensing, intuiting, thinking, and feeling, Mok described communication patterns associated with each function. His work focuses on the importance of understanding these communication patterns in relating to clients, in working effectively as management teams, and in diverse applications such as marketing, sales, and personnel work.

With his model as a basis, two educators, Anita Simon and Claudia Byram (1977), identified the importance of communication patterns for teachers working with students, parents, administrators, and with each other. In their book, *You've Got to Reach 'Em to Teach'Em,* they describe the importance of knowing one's own style, of knowing how to style-flex, and of applying a knowledge of students' styles to instruction, discipline, parent conferencing, motivation, rewards, and evaluation.

The continuing work of these and other researchers and practitioners makes the original theories of Carl Jung important and practical for educators to understand and use.

Communicating with Style

What happens at a school when people recognize differences in style and are willing and able to deal with them? First and foremost, diversity of human personality is accepted as the norm. Administrators, teachers, students, and parents are expected to be different. When we expect people to be different, we tune into people's assumptions about issues, problems, and questions. We ask "How would Dale approach this?" "What will David think about this?" "How would Jane solve this problem?" "What would be best for this student?"

Perhaps more importantly, we stop the futile search for the one right answer to issues and problems in education. There cannot be one best way to run schools, a right way to design a report card or a teacher evaluation, a best reading text for every student, a best physical design for a classroom, or of course, a best way to teach. When we accept diversity as the norm we recognize that things that work extremely well for some students, for some teachers, and for some administrators will not necessarily work best for others. This is a fundamental change in thinking. It is a change that leads us to celebrate and use the diversity within schools rather than to ignore or attempt to eliminate it. Roland Barth (1980) described this challenge in the story of his job as principal of a public elementary school:

Diversity is abundant and free. Used wisely, deliberately, and constructively, it offers an untapped, renewable resource available to the public schools. We should learn to use it well (p. 16).

Perhaps one of the most important applications of style awareness in the human-relations area is the self-knowledge that we gain by recognizing our own perspective on the world. We begin to consciously identify our strengths, and use the skills they give us. At the same time we can identify our weaker areas and recognize the importance of compensating for them through changes in our own behavior or collaboration with other people. Developing self-awareness without the judgmental labels of "right" or "wrong" or "best" or "better" can bring us a positive sense of self-esteem. As professional educators we can respect the variety of approaches that our colleagues bring to the teaching/learning situation, learn from them, but at the same time be comfortable with the skills our own strengths give us. Teachers and administrators in our classes and workshops often say that the best part of learning about style is knowing that "I'm OK!"

In schools where diversity is accepted as the norm and where the belief that people are different is taken seriously, conscious style-flexing is practiced every day. Style-flexing implies knowing not only our own style but our impact on others. As a person with a strong thinking pattern, for example, I have to know that some people see me as too attentive to detail, too bogged down in nitty-gritty facts, and as very slow to come to decisions. While I value my accuracy and exactness, another person may see me as being extremely fastidious and picayune. While I value my thorough planning, another person may see me as being rigid. While I value my objectivity and control over emotion, another person may see me as cold and impersonal. Knowing that differences in style affect not only my own behavior but also how others see me helps me understand how to better communicate with people. When I know I am having a certain impact on others I can become conscious of how to relate positively to them. This involves knowing their needs.

For example, as a dominant-thinking administrator talking to a sensing teacher about a child with a special need, I can get to the point early on in the conversation by giving him or her the conclusion I have reached and then asking the teacher to listen to my reasoning behind it. I can talk to the feeling teacher by focusing on the emotional impact on the child, and then ask him or her to examine the data I used to arrive at my decision. I can talk to the intuiting teacher by first asking for his or her suggestions and ideas and then together examining the data I have compiled.

When I understand the styles of others, I can use my own and others' strengths to work together for the best results. What this implies, of course, is some modification of my own behavior but not necessarily a change in my basic beliefs or philosophy. It is a conscious adaptation of my behavior in order to facilitate positive communication.

Another example of style-flexing at work is at a conference between an administrator, a teacher, and a parent to address the issue of whether to retain a child in the same grade for the next school year. Assume that the parent exhibits a strong feeling style and focuses on the emotional effect this decision will have on the child. When the parent comes from this perspective, it will not be helpful for the teacher to refer to the grade book and go through a careful analysis of the child's marks on the quizzes and exams. Nor will it be helpful for the administrator to pull out the SAT scores and show curves illustrating the child's standing in relation to the rest of the class. What the parent most needs is to discuss the emotional impact the decision is going to have on the child. Both the teacher and administrator can help the parent focus on the academic areas as they relate to the child's emotional well-being. Comments such as, "It must be hard for Trisha to have to struggle academically," and "Trisha often seems to feel tense during quizzes in class" are going to be much more appropriate and helpful than comments that directly relate to the objective data.

In this example, the best decision for the child will be made when the parent, the teacher, and the administrator communicate positively. The child will benefit by the collective wisdom of these people with their different perspectives on the problem. The decision to retain a child should include an analytical review of achievement as well as consideration of the emotional impact.

In this kind of situation, and the many greater and smaller ones that occur every day in schools, an understanding of the diversity of human nature and an acceptance of it as the norm can result in a cooperative attitude toward decisions and problems. Schools that celebrate diversity among people will be able to use this strength to produce effective learning.

4. Supervision and Evaluation
Witkin's Field-Dependence-Independence

A trifling matter, and fussy of me, but we all have our little ways.

> —Eeyore to Pooh
> A. A. Milne
> *The House At Pooh Corner*

"Good job, Kathy," Barney Quinn, the principal, comments after dropping in on Kathy's language-arts class.

Later that day, Kathy is talking with her friend and fellow teacher, Gordon. "Good job! Can you imagine? What kind of comment is that? And he just dropped in! I wonder if he thinks this will count as an official observation?"

"Relax, Kathy," Gordon responds, "that's Barney—he often drops in. It's his way of keeping in touch. I like those visits; they take the pressure off the 'official' observations. Be complimented that he said 'Good job!' He means it."

WHEN TEACHERS AND ADMINISTRATORS TALK ABOUT SUPERVISION AND EVALUATION, they bring their own set of values to these concepts. For some administrators supervision and evaluation are ongoing functions related to all their interactions with staff. These administrators feel that their role as instructional leaders includes a pervasive, low-key, continual supervision of staff. Other administrators pride themselves on the separation of evaluation from other interactions with staff. They carefully schedule evaluative observations and stick to specific objective criteria. In the final analysis, various approaches to supervision and evaluation will work if the administrator is skilled at whatever approach he or she takes. But the approach—the style—will elicit a different reaction from different staff, as illustrated above with Kathy and Gordon's comments.

Teachers, too, bring their own styles to issues of supervision and evaluation. Some prefer the casual drop-in approach; others want a formal schedule. Some value specific criteria in a checklist form. Others rebel at this approach, asking, "How could those lists capture the real strengths of my teaching?"

Again, the issue is not one of right or wrong but a matter of style. If teachers want an administrator to drop in regularly to get a sense of the positive climate of their classes, which they work hard to develop, that will be more important than the comments about an observation of a specific math lesson. But a teacher who feels that specific instructional skills are the most important indication of competency will want the administrator to formally evaluate a lesson. Comments about the students' relationships with each other in this class will simply not be as important.

Administrators and teachers need to be aware of these style differences in approaches to, and expectations of, supervision and evaluation. To discuss a specific example, we will focus on the cognitive style dimension of field-dependence-independence described by the late Herman A. Witkin and his colleagues. As you read, remember that other style models could as easily be applied to this important area and that the Witkin model has many applications to other areas of education.

Field-Dependence-Independence—Herman A. Witkin

Can you find this isolated figure

in this more complex figure?

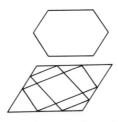

It takes some people as little as three seconds to perform the task, while others, with similar intelligence, search for several minutes and cannot locate the isolated figure. What about you?

People vary in their abilities to differentiate objects from their backgrounds. This difference in perception can be extreme: A highly differentiated, field-independent person will succeed quickly no matter how difficult the problem, whereas an extremely field-dependent person often needs to have the figure pointed out. Most of us lean toward one or the other of these poles; we differ in the time it takes us to complete the task and the complexity of problems we are able to solve. This perceptual characteristic of field dependency, originally labeled cognitive style, has been linked to learning, teaching, and many other behaviors.

The above figure, and others like it, are included in the Group Embedded Figures Test (Oltman et al., 1971), which is derived from the work of Herman Witkin. In the latter half of the 1940s, Witkin and his associates began exploring distinctive perceptual characteristics among people. The researchers were interested in knowing to what extent a person's perception of an item was influenced by the context ("field") in which it appeared. In other words, were there people who saw the tree while others saw the forest?

Early in his work, Witkin sought to determine why some pilots became disoriented and actually flew their planes upside down when they lost sight of the ground. In order to assess a person's perception of his or her own orientation in space, an experiment was devised in which the subject was seated in a moving chair, which was to be brought to true upright regardless of the slant of a small "room" surrounding the chair. Similar experiments were conducted in which the subject was to locate a rod upright in the space of a frame. Both rod and frame could be tilted independently and were lighted while surrounding darkness eliminated other visual distractions.

These and other experiments led Witkin and his associates to define two extreme indicators of the extent to which the surrounding organized field influences an observer's perception of an item within it. A person with a *field-dependent* (FD) mode of perception is strongly influenced by the prevailing field, while the *field-independent* (FI) person experiences items as more or less separate from the surrounding field. Thus the field-independent person is successful in attaining a correct upright placement of the chair and the rod in the above experiments by ignoring the surrounding room or frame. A field-dependent person, however, will align the chair on the rod more in relationship to the external clue (room or frame) and insist that it is upright. Most subjects tested scored along a continuum from FI to FD, tending toward one or the other pole.

Later, Witkin expanded his studies into different aspects of personality.

He explored what the people clustering together near each pole have in common. Can people with FD and FI perception be expected to have certain consistent characteristics? Over time, Witkin and his associates became convinced that the field-dependence-independence dimension influences one's perceptual and intellectual domains as well as personality traits such as social behavior, body concept, and defenses. The results of more than 35 years of research, providing a rich and useful font of information, are compiled in bibliographies listing over 2,000 studies (Witkin et al., 1973).

Since Witkin's concern was primarily psychological research, educators have to examine his work thoughtfully to develop ways it can be properly applied to the educational setting. A solid research base exists for the field-dependent-independent concepts, but a wider knowledge and application of Witkin's work within educational circles is lacking. Witkin recognized the importance of his research for educators and prepared an extensive article on this aspect of his work (Witkin et al., 1977). We compiled information from this article and adapted it for educational applications in the descriptions of learners in Figure 4 and of teachers in Figure 5, pages 30-31.

Diagnosis of adults and students for field-dependence-independence is now possible with validated paper-and-pencil instrumentation. One of these instruments, the Embedded Figures Test (Witkin, 1969), is administered individually and takes about 30 minutes. Another instrument that has been widely used is the Group Embedded Figures Test mentioned above. This instrument is valid for ages 11 and above and can be administered to a group in 20 minutes. There is also a children's version of the instrument for youngsters between the ages of five and ten (Karp and Konstadt, 1971), and a preschool version for children three to five years (Coates, 1972).

Witkin's work has a variety of messages for educators. His studies have consistently demonstrated cognitive styles to be independent of intelligence, and thus "field-dependence-independence appears to be more related to the 'how' than to the 'how much' of cognitive function" (Witkin et al., 1977:24). Since cognitive style is neutral, both field-dependent and field-independent people, according to studies, make good students and good teachers. However, since style does affect success in specific kinds of situations, as illustrated in the chart, educators must be sensitive to style-related demands in teaching and learning.

In offering advice to educators for responding to cognitive style differences, Witkin urges us to consider the advantages of both matching and mismatching. He points out that the "development of greater diversity in behaviors within individuals seems as important an objective as the recognition

Figure 4. How Students Learn	
Field Dependence	**Field Independence**
Perceive globally	Perceive analytically
Experience in a global fashion, adhere to structures as given	Experience in an articulated fashion, impose structure or restrictions
Make broad general distinctions among concepts, see relationships	Make specific concept distinctions, see little overlap
Have a social orientation to the world	Have an impersonal orientation to the world
Learn material with social content best	Learn social material only as an intentional task
Attend best to material relevant to own experience	Interested in new concepts for their own sake
Seek externally defined goals and reinforcements	Have self-defined goals and reinforcements
Want organization to be provided	Can self-structure situations
More affected by criticism	Less affected by criticism
Use spectator approach to concept attainment	Use hypothesis testing approach to attain concepts

and the utilization of diversity among individuals" (1977:53). Ultimately, he wants knowledge of field-dependence-independence to contribute to the teachers' and students' abilities to use their own style strengths and then develop more diverse strategies to facilitate success in learning.

Style-Sensitive Supervision

What does this mean in terms of supervision and evaluation? As we've studied personality characteristics associated with Witkin's style patterns and talked with teachers and administrators about their styles, we've been able to develop some generalizations about supervision and evaluation. Figure 6 represents some typical expectations that teachers of different styles have for administrators, and Figure 7 (p. 32) identifies some general con-

Figure 5. How Teachers Teach

Field Dependence	Field Independence
Strong in establishing a warm and personal learning environment, emphasize personal aspects of instruction	Strong in organizing and guiding student learning, emphasize cognitive aspect of instruction
Prefer teaching situations that allow interaction and discussion with students	Prefer impersonal teaching methods such as lecture and problem solving
Use questions to check on student learning following instruction	Use questions to introduce topics and following student answers
More student-centered	More teacher-centered
Provide less feedback, avoid negative evaluation	Give specific corrective feedback, use negative evaluation

cerns about evaluation. As with all dichotomous lists, there is seldom a pure fit, but most people identify more with one style than the other.

What happens in a school that attends to style in the areas of supervision and evaluation? First and foremost, the people involved understand each other in a more realistic and profound way. A teacher, for example,

Figure 6. What Teachers Expect From An Administrator

Field Dependence	Field Independence
To give warmth, personal interest, support	To focus on tasks
To provide guidance, to model	To allow independence and flexibility
To seek their opinions in making decisions	To make decisions based on analysis of the problem
To like them	To be knowledgeable about curriculum and instruction
To have an open door	To maintain professional distance
To "practice what they preach"	To be professionally experienced in appropriate content areas
To use tones and body language to support words	To give messages directly and articulately

---

Figure 7. How Teachers Want to be Evaluated	
Field Dependence	**Field Independence**
With an emphasis on class "climate," interpersonal relationships, and quality of student-teacher interaction	With an emphasis on accuracy of content, adherence to learning objectives and assessment of learnings
With a narrative report and personal discussion	With a specific list of criteria
With consideration of student and parent comments	With consideration of academic achievement and test scores
With credit for "effort" and for trying	With evidence and facts to support comments

knows "where an administrator is coming from" when he or she says "good job." A principal hears a teacher's "Just drop in any time" with a deeper understanding. This mutual awareness can help focus the supervisory and evaluative process on professional growth.

At the same time, awareness of style will help educators respond to each other's needs in evaluation and supervision. An administrator will understand that some teachers need specific time commitments for evaluative visits and clear objective criteria. Others on the staff may want and need a more casual observation schedule with more focus on the less tangible aspects of teaching, such as climate, student relationships, and motivation. When administrators and teachers understand each other's needs, they can use the supervisory process to take advantage of each other's strengths.

Understanding style in relationship to supervision can help administrators and teachers accept the value of multiple criteria for evaluation. They can consciously focus on the objective parts of instruction and curriculum and on the more subjective affective areas. At the same time, wise administrators and teachers will encourage diversity in the methods that are used in supervision and evaluation—seeking opportunities for clinical supervision, for peer coaching among staff, for objective-based checklists, and for narrative reports. In his recent proposal for differentiated supervision, Allan Glatthorn (1984) urges that "Teachers should have some choice about the kind of supervision they receive—in contrast to the situation that prevails in most schools" (p. 1).

Finally, supervision and evaluation that actively consider individual needs of the people involved can result in professional growth rather than being just tasks to be gotten through. It is always easier to accept suggestions from those with whom we share mutual respect. If we hear another's comments from the perspective of a different set of values, it is difficult to internalize them for our own growth. On the other hand, when someone seems to "understand me," I am more willing to accept his or her perspective. This openness helps me to listen, so that I really hear and can incorporate the suggestions in my professional work.

Educators who value individual differences must model that value in relationships with each other. Teachers and administrators who respect each others' styles can help one another to improve through the supervisory process.

5. Teaching Style
Gregorc's Mediation Abilities

Understanding one's own magical mystery is one of the teacher's most important assets if he is to understand that everyone is thus differently equipped.

—Buckminster Fuller

The Schimmels have just moved to town, and today they are visiting the local elementary school their children will be attending. The principal, Mr. Areglado, has welcomed them and given them a schedule for their various classroom visitations. After several hours they return to his office, feeling generally positive about the school but somewhat confused about the teaching differences they saw in the classrooms. They ask Mr. Areglado to tell them a little bit more about the school.

He begins by explaining that the basic philosophy of the school is to meet the needs of all children and to provide the best programs possible to help each child succeed. The Schimmels couldn't agree more, but why then did they see such different things going on in the classrooms? "Aren't there some basic rules about good teaching that guide the school?" "Yes, of course," Mr. Areglado answers and then adds that the school believes in respecting and, as a matter of fact, encouraging diversity among its teaching staff. This diversity leads to a greater ability to meet the needs of the individual students who attend the school, he says. "Let me tell you about some of the teachers to give you an example," Mr. Areglado begins.

"Mrs. R. is the senior member of our staff. She has been teaching here for more than 20 years. She's warm, personable, and caring, and these qualities are immediately apparent in her relationships with the children and in the atmosphere she sets in her classroom. She personalizes her curriculum by responding to the interests of her students and sharing her own

interests. Children and parents respond enthusiastically to her as a person and children are successful in her room.

"Mr. D. across the hall is one of the newest teachers on our staff. He is a very active, project-oriented person. He has a lot of hobbies and is very skilled with his hands. He'll often build curriculum materials for the children to use, and he encourages them to do active projects to express their learning. He has a marvelous ability to make abstract ideas realistic for children and to relate learning to their everyday lives. Parents often find themselves roped into projects to help him and the children work on curriculum. The bottom line, of course, is that through active involvement in projects, children are developing their skills.

"Down the hall you visited our team-teaching classroom. Mrs. S. and Miss J. have been working together for the past three years. They enjoy this arrangement because they find that sharing the curriculum gives them an opportunity to become more or less experts in a few areas. Miss J. handles all of the reading, and she's marvelous at bringing a variety of approaches to helping the children learn to read. Several years ago she finished her master's degree in reading, and she continues to update herself regularly by taking courses at the local university. I've seen some children gain several years in their reading skills under her guidance. Mrs. S. is equally enthusiastic about mathematics. She has a marvelous ability to make children excited about math skills as well as concepts. Best of all, of course, these two teachers plan the curriculum together, and they use their skills to complement each other.

"I could go on about all of the other members of the staff. The point, Mr. and Mrs. Schimmel, is that we have a very strong, but very diverse staff. Our parents have come to enjoy that aspect of our school, and they look forward to their children having different approaches as they move through the grades. Why don't you tell me a little bit more about your children and what you hope for them so that I can recommend an appropriate placement?"

CAN THE ABOVE SCENARIO WORK? CAN A SCHOOL SUCCESSFULLY EDUCATE CHILdren by allowing and even encouraging a great deal of diversity among its staff? Is it possible that having a diversity of teaching styles might actually be the best way to run a school? Roland Barth (1980), one principal who believes so, has described his experiences in his book, *Run School Run*. "I have found that when teachers are teaching in ways consonant with their own personal style and professional philosophy, both they and their students appear to benefit" (p. 15).

When we accept that people are really different, we must also accept that teachers will certainly bring their own uniqueness to the way they teach. We call this "teaching style." The personality of each individual and unique teacher will be reflected in his or her professional behavior. We will see differences in the way teachers relate to students. We will see differences in how teachers structure and manage their classrooms. We will see differences in the mood and tone that teachers set in their classrooms. We will see differences in the methods and materials teachers use to help students learn. We will see differences in curriculum interests and emphases. We will see differences in expectations for student work and in teachers' priorities and strategies for evaluation of student learning. All of these are manifestations of the teacher's individual style.

Teaching style governs the reality of the classroom. No two teachers will use a program or text in exactly the same way. Each teacher personally makes the curriculum come alive for students. The individual teacher conveys attitudes toward content and processes. John Goodlad (1984) calls the teacher "coach, quarterback, referee, and even rule-maker" (p. 108). In his extensive study of schools he found that

The classroom is indeed the teacher's domain, and here, according to our data, teachers perceive themselves to be quite autonomous. Our teachers saw themselves to be in control of what they taught, and how. ...Approximately two-thirds of the teachers at all levels perceived that they had complete "control" in their selection of teaching techniques and students' learning activities (pp. 188-189).

When we accept that teaching styles exist and that the individual teacher has a great deal of autonomy, we then have to make a decision to encourage or discourage individual styles, to encourage diversity or encourage uniformity. We need to decide *when* teachers need to be similar and *when* they can be different. When making this decision, it is important to remember the previous comments about the difference between style and competence. There certainly are specific identifiable teaching competencies. Effective teachers need to have clear purposes and objectives. They need to be able to use effective instructional methods and techniques, to motivate and support students in appropriate ways, to monitor instruction, and to assess and evaluate the effectiveness of the learning. The question of teaching style is whether it is possible, and even desirable, for teachers to exhibit these teaching competencies in a variety of individual ways.

In Ted Sizer's (1984) report on high schools, he describes three different successful teachers and attributes their success to their judgment, which he sees as an extension of their personalities. "One visits classes and sometimes see experts, each with his or her own special style," he notes (p. 153). Sizer concludes his study with a number of imperatives for better schools. The first is: "Give room to teachers and students to work and learn in their own, appropriate ways" (p. 214).

To look at a specific example of teaching style, we will discuss the work of Anthony Gregorc. Again, Gregorc's work is one example of a way to understand teaching style. We could apply the same principles and comments about teaching style to the work of other researchers and use Gregorc's model in other areas of education.

Mediation Abilities—Anthony F. Gregorc

Gregorc says that his interest in style emanated from an understanding of his own comfort and discomfort in a variety of jobs he held in education as a teacher, administrator, and college professor. He also considered his practical experiences with students in a high school for exceptional children, where he and the staff observed an unevenness in children's successes. The subjective personal experiences and objective professional experiences led Gregorc to identify and examine the notion of individual differences in an applied and philosophical way. Throughout his work, this balance of the practical, the philosophical, and the psychological is always apparent. It brings depth to his model. For Gregorc, the style reflected in our behavior is an indication of the qualities of our mind. He thus identifies style patterns in the context of total view of life, which he calls the "Organon System."

> ... the primary purpose of life is to realize and actualize one's individuality, spirituality, and collective humanness. ... The ORGANON System is an organized viewpoint of how and why the human mind functions and manifests itself through the human personality. [It studies] two mediation abilities of the mind: perception and ordering (Gregorc, 1982, p. v., emphasis in original).

When we perceive, our mind has a tendency to "see" things in a mental, symbolic, intuitive, and emotional way and to "see" things in a realistic, direct, physical way. These different kinds of perception, abstract or concrete, describe opposite ends of a continuum.

Abstract ——————————————————————— *Concrete*

Every person is capable of using abstract and concrete perception, but we each have a tendency to prefer one over the other.

The mind also exhibits an ability to order information, knowledge, ideas and concepts. Sometimes it orders things in a linear, step-by-step, and methodical way. At other times, it orders in a nonlinear, tangential and leaping way. These two kinds of ordering, sequential or random, form opposite ends of a continuum.

Sequential ————————————————————— *Random*

While every person is able to use both sequential and random ordering, we each have a tendency to prefer and to operate most frequently and most successfully with one kind of ordering.

Combining both perception and ordering, Gregorc identifies four distinct patterns of style. Some people will perceive in a concrete way and order with a sequential pattern, thus exhibiting a *Concrete Sequential* (CS) style. Others will perceive in an abstract way and then order sequentially, resulting in an *Abstract Sequential* (AS) style. Some will perceive in a concrete way and then order what has been perceived in a random way, producing the *Concrete Random* (CR) style. And finally, those who perceive in an abstract way and order randomly will be identified as having an *Abstract Random* (AR) style.

"The Gregorc Style Delineator" (Gregorc, 1982) is a self-analysis tool designed to assess a person's perceptual and ordering-mediation abilities.

Fig. 8

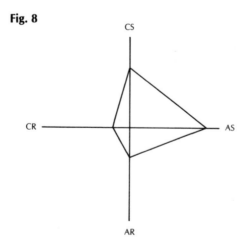

Sets of words are ranked, and a numerical score is obtained for each of the four patterns. The scores are then plotted on a grid that produces a four-pointed shape. Strong preference for one style over the other three will produce a very dramatic point toward that part of the grid.

The resulting visual picture of the relationship of the four style scores is very effective in helping us to keep in mind that there will always be an interaction of different stylistic characteristics in our behavior. A person with a dominant AS style and a strong CS back-up style would have a profile similar to that shown in Fig. 8.

Mediation Abilities and Teaching Style

Kathleen Butler (1984), a colleague of Gregorc, offers a comprehensive definition of teaching style:

Each teacher brings a unique self to the classroom. The strength of our personal goals, expressed through natural style, pulls in a fairly consistent direction and creates our view of what teaching can and should be. *Teaching style is a set of attitudes and actions that open a formal and informal world of learning to students. It is a subtle force that influences student access to learning and teaching by establishing perimeters around acceptable learning procedures, processes, and products. The powerful force of the teacher's attitude toward students as well as the instructional activities used by the teacher shape the learning/teaching experience and require of the teacher and student certain mediation abilities and capacities. Thus, the manner in which teachers present themselves as human beings and receive learners as human beings is as influential upon the students' lives and learning as the daily activities in the classroom* (pp.51- 52, emphasis in original).

Let us look at how the mediation abilities described in Gregorc's model will be reflected in a teacher's style. A teacher who prefers concrete perception and sequential ordering will exhibit the Concrete Sequential style in his or her teaching. This teacher will be practical, will use hands-on learning experiences, plan field-trips, enjoy projects, and have a variety of manipulative materials available in the classroom. When parents, like the Schimmels at the beginning of the chapter, visit this teacher's classroom, they will see a utilitarian environment with schedules, fire-drill procedures, and the daily bulletin posted. Students will be expected to be task-oriented and to complete their work by showing all the steps. The CS teacher will appreciate specific order and routines and will manage the classroom in a structured and logical way. These teachers have special abilities to make school practical, realistic, predictable and secure for students.

When a teacher perceives in an abstract way and then orders sequentially, he or she will have an Abstract Sequential teaching style. Teachers who prefer this style will apply their logical and sequential reasoning to abstract ideas and to symbols, theories, and concepts. They will encourage students to be analytical, to evaluate what they are learning, and to support their ideas with logical evidence and data. When the Schimmel family visits this teacher's class, they might see students doing research in an impersonal, structured setting. These teachers have a deep respect for depth of knowledge and expertise and will expect students to exhibit good study skills. Gathering accurate information is very important for learning in their classrooms, and there will be many abstract resources available, especially books, for students to use. These teachers are wonderful at encouraging students to be intellectually curious and to rigorously build a broad base of knowledge.

When a teacher perceives in an abstract way but then orders randomly, he or she will have an Abstract Random teaching style. Teachers who prefer this style rely on personal understanding of curriculum and content. They focus on individual students, their interests, and their needs, and they design the classroom experiences in a very child-centered way. They respond perceptively to the moods and tones of the class and behave spontaneously when something of interest to themselves or the students occurs. They enjoy artistic and creative activities, projects, and materials. When the Schimmels visit this classroom, they will see children's work displayed and colorful mood-setting posters reflecting the teacher's and students' interests. These teachers see their job as educating the whole child. They strive to develop esteem and self-confidence and require students to cooperate and share. They make the content in the classroom personal and seek to suit the curriculum to the individual as much as possible. They focus on relationships by teaching knowledge and skills through themes. These teachers are often inspiring and help students bring joy and enthusiasm to learning.

Finally, when a teacher perceives in a concrete way and orders randomly, he or she will have a Concrete Random teaching style. Teachers who prefer this style emphasize practical, realistic work but want it expressed in original and creative ways. They encourage students to invent and problem solve by producing products that are both useful and original. These teachers are active, enthusiastic, flexible, and spontaneous in the classroom. They are resourceful, use a variety of methods, change often, and, of course, promote active student involvement. They love to experiment, and they encourage students to make choices, think for themselves, and ask "Why?" When the Schimmels visit, they will see a busy environment without an immediately apparent order, and with a variety of students' work in various stages of completion. These teachers "challenge students to move beyond given knowledge and traditional learning to discover new ideas and products for themselves" (Butler, 1984, p. 107). They are wonderful catalysts, encouraging both students and fellow staff members to view learning as a constantly challenging adventure.

Within each of these descriptions of teaching styles there would be individual diversity, because each teacher's primary style would be affected by strengths in other style areas. Still, on a visit to almost any school, examples can be found of each of these teaching styles.

Teaching With Style

Working with the concept of teaching style implies celebrating and using the diversity of teachers' differences. It means encouraging each teacher to work with his or her strengths; actively using the diversity among the staff in curriculum planning and schoolwide decision making; maintaining a balance of styles in staffing the school as a whole and in staffing individual departments and grade levels, and respecting the notion of style in planning for growth for individual teachers and for improvement in the school programs.

A school that celebrates diversity of teaching style will encourage CS teachers in their practical structured approaches, will applaud AR teachers for their personal warmth and spontaneity, will be grateful for the enthusiasm and experimentation of CR teachers, and will welcome the intellectual rigor that AS teachers bring. In such a school, decisions about programs and organization will be made by using the strengths of these different styles.

Curriculum committees will be formed to consciously maximize the diversity, so that different perspectives will be brought to the final recommendations and products. Teachers will be encouraged to learn from each other while also respecting each other's differences. It will be accepted that students will respond to teachers in different ways, and student placement will take this into consideration. The value of matching a student with a like teacher will be used when appropriate, but at the same time students will be encouraged to grow and stretch by working with a teacher who is stylistically different from themselves.

Specific teaching competencies will be defined, and teachers will be encouraged to evaluate their competencies in light of their own styles. Growth will be expected from each teacher but without comparison with another person whose style is different. When each teacher, individually or in conjunction with a supervisor, plans for personal growth, particular stylistic strengths and potential problems will be a key focus. The administrator will work with each person to validate strengths, to plan for ways to minimize weaknesses, and to develop new skills. CS teachers will be encouraged to develop a higher tolerance for spontaneity and to avoid being too rigid and inflexible in their expectations and structures. AS teachers will be urged to make learning practical and to value emotional responses from students. AR teachers will need to examine their potential for overpersonalization of curriculum and relationships with students. And the CR teachers will be encouraged to maintain appropriate routines and respect proven traditions.

A school that uses and celebrates diversity in teaching style creates an opportunity for all students to find their styles accommodated at some time and in some classrooms. Teachers will know that students can and do learn in different ways because they will see their colleagues using a variety of strategies to produce success for students. They also will be aware of the different models of teaching among each other enabling them to develop more diverse teaching strategies. Parents will view the school as offering a variety of options for their children and will also know through practical experience that children can and do learn from different teaching approaches.

Perhaps most importantly, because these teachers experience respect for their own individuality, they will in turn feel comfortable to convey this respect for uniqueness in their relationships with students.

6. Counseling

Dunn and Dunn's Learning Style Elements

Try to see it my way,
Only time will tell if I'm right or I am wrong,
While you see it your way,
There's a chance that we may fall apart before
too long.
We can work it out.
We can work it out.

—John Lennon and Paul McCartney

COUNSELING OFFICE, END OF FIRST QUARTER:

Susan is in your office because she is not doing well in school. Not doing well translates to a 1.3 grade-point average out of a possible 4.0. She is a bit tense, sitting and fidgeting. After the preliminaries, you get to the crux of the matter by asking Susan what she feels is causing the difficulty with her schoolwork.

"I have the ability, but I don't apply myself," she replies.

With this reply two things may race through the counselor's mind: first, Susan has been counseled before; and second, she just said what you were going to say!

After reassuring her that what she said is indeed true, you encourage her to study harder and perhaps talk about the need for good grades to keep from closing off options in the future. Then you send her back to class.

COUNSELING OFFICE, END OF SECOND QUARTER:

Susan is in your office because she is not doing well in school. Not doing well translates to a 1.3 grade point average of a possible 4.0. She is a

---

bit tense, sitting and fidgeting. After the preliminaries, you get to the crux of the matter by asking Susan what she feels is causing the difficulty with her schoolwork.

"I have the ability, but I don't apply myself," she replies.

At this point the whole situation begins to seem vaguely familiar. Once more you reassure her that she does indeed have the ability, and you again tell her to study harder. Only this time there is an important difference: You say it louder and slower—almost in the same way you would give directions to a person who has difficulty understanding the language you are speaking.

ALTHOUGH THE ABOVE SCENARIO MAY SOMETIMES BE ALL TOO REAL, IT IS MEANT TO exaggerate what often transpires in the counselor's office. How can we change this pattern?

Knowledge of styles may offer a student like Susan some concrete ways to improve her learning efficiency. It can help open up a dialogue with the student and help her to view the counselor as a part of a "learning team." It can encourage students to take tentative first steps toward accepting responsibility for their learning. Knowing their individual styles will not make students more intelligent, but by approaching learning more efficiently, students can better cope with the demands of school by knowing how to maximize the intellectual gifts available to them.

The researchers chosen for this application example are Rita and Kenneth Dunn. The reader is reminded that the work of any of the researchers on style could appear in this section, just as the Dunns' model can be used effectively in other application areas.

Learning Style Elements—Rita Dunn and Kenneth Dunn

Rita and Kenneth Dunn are perhaps the best-known researchers of learning styles. They publish widely in education journals, have written a number of books, and present seminars on learning styles across the country.

The Dunns (1975a: 74) describe learning styles as "the manner in which at least 18 different elements of four basic stimuli affect a person's ability to absorb and to retain information, values, facts or concepts." The four basic stimuli are environmental, emotional, sociological, and physical. The elements of each are illustrated in Figure 9.

In order to question the student for the above factors, the Dunns, work-

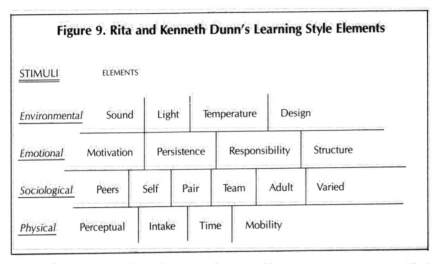

Figure 9. Rita and Kenneth Dunn's Learning Style Elements

STIMULI	ELEMENTS			
Environmental	Sound	Light	Temperature	Design
Emotional	Motivation	Persistence	Responsibility	Structure
Sociological	Peers	Self	Pair	Team	Adult	Varied
Physical	Perceptual	Intake	Time	Mobility

ing with statistician Gary Price, evolved a self-reporting instrument called the Learning Styles Inventory (LSI). It is available in three different forms: for grades 3-5; grades 6-12; and in an adult version, called the Productivity Environmental Preference Survey (PEPS).

Administration of the instrument is straightforward and convenient. The person taking the grade 6-12 LSI is given five possible choices in response to each of 104 questions: the respondent may strongly disagree, disagree, be unsure, agree, or strongly agree. Following are some sample questions from the grades 6-12 instrument:

1. I study best when it is quiet.
2. I like to make my parents happy by getting good grades.
3. I like studying with lots of light.
4. I like to be told exactly what to do.
5. I concentrate best when I feel warm.

The responses can be computer scored, and the resulting printout indicates which of the elements are important factors in the person's learning. With this convenient reference, a teacher can focus the learning style of each student throughout the day and confirm the inventory profile with observations of classroom behaviors.

In addition to the individual student profiles, the computer scoring services can also provide the teacher with a group summary sheet. This allows the classroom teacher to quickly determine those students in the class with certain learning style preferences without having to examine each student's individual profile. Common class patterns will emerge, and the teacher can adapt methods, physical environment, and groups to accommodate the students. In one example, by referring to the group summary sheet, the teacher can know which of the students need quiet as opposed to those who prefer sound in the background as they learn. In another instance, if it is "always the same students who are out of their seats," the teacher may find that those are the students who show a preference for mobility. Likewise, the students who are "always talking" may very well be those whose LSI results indicate a preference for learning in a team or with a peer.

With careful study of the Dunns' model a teacher can begin to devise ways in which the individual needs of the students in the class can be recognized and acted upon. At the very least, knowing students' learning preferences can make the teacher more sensitive to the individual differences of the people in the class. This increased sensitivity on the teacher's part will make it easier for that teacher to view some student actions—for example, being out of their seats—as an expression of student individuality as it relates to learning rather than as a threat to the teacher's authority or ability to maintain classroom discipline. The teacher can then respond to the student's behavior with a recognition that the action may be an expression of how the student learns, and may then provide the student with a strategy that responds to the student's individual preference.

Along with the valuable information provided about the individual student, the practicality and ease of the administration and scoring of the LSI makes the Dunns' research appealing and has led to its wide use. Teachers in many schools have received inservice on the Dunns' model and, after administering the LSI, have begun adapting their teaching in conjunction with the results that the instrument generated. In one example, at O'Dea High School in Seattle, the Dunns' research was used in the area of counseling. Teachers, parents, and students were given inservice about learning styles. The LSI was then administered to each of the students in the freshman class, and the student profile was placed in each student's file and referred to as necessary. Each freshman teacher received a group summary sheet, and each student received a copy of the profile.

The Dunns complement the widespread application of their model with continued research into the area of learning style. Rita Dunn is a professor at St. John's University, New York, and the school has become a center for research on styles. In a recent survey of the research (1982), she cites studies confirming that

1. students can identify their own strong style preferences;

2. teaching through learning styles increases academic achievement and improves students' attitudes toward school; and

3. learning style is often stable over time and consistent across subject areas.

The Dunns were also instrumental in beginning the *Learning Styles Network Newsletter,* a publication with articles concerning learning styles research, applications, and reviews of books on styles. The *Newsletter* provides a forum for researchers and practitioners to report on implementation of learning styles concepts in various parts of the country. This reporting allows the subscriber to get in contact with the people applying the styles concepts and makes it possible to build on prior research.

The Learning Style Center in St. John's University offers training and materials designed to respond to student learning style differences. The Dunns and their associates have developed Contract Activity Packages and a variety of other resources for application in the classroom. Their training workshops guide teachers in diagnostic-prescriptive process to develop strategies and materials for meeting needs of various learners.

Counseling with Style

With the Dunns' profile of learning style, a counselor has something of substance on which to base the meeting with the student who is not performing well in school. Studying the student's learning style printout prior to meeting with the student, the counselor can prepare for the interview. For example, the counselor could ask Susan (who "has the ability but doesn't apply herself") to describe how she studies when she has something important to learn. She may respond that she sits at the desk her parents bought her when she began high school and studies under a high- intensity light for two hours each evening, just prior to supper.

Reviewing her computer printout beforehand may reveal that Susan prefers informal design (meaning she prefers to study on the floor, couch, bed, etc.) and likes dim lighting where she studies. The LSI printout may also reveal that Susan's best time to study may be the evening—after supper—and not in the late afternoon, when she is currently hitting the books. Thus, through the process of studying the Dunns' instrument and interviewing the student, it is possible to identify some things that may actually be inhibiting the student and things which, if done differently, may make Susan more efficient with her studies. For example, she may be a more efficient learner if she were to forsake the desk, high intensity light, and before-supper sessions in order to study under low light while lying on the carpet sometime after dinner.

Another item that may emerge from Susan's profile is that she is not persistent. An experienced counselor with this information will realize that a nonpersistent person cannot study for two straight hours each night. The counselor may ask Susan to describe what she does for those two hours at her desk. It is possible that Susan will relate that she spends two hours in her room studying, but as the conversation progresses she will begin to realize that a good portion of the time is being spent in other activities, for example reading magazines or writing notes to friends. In terms of prescription it may be more realistic at this point to ask the nonpersistent Susan if she thinks she can study for 15 minutes, then take a break, and return some time later for another 15 minutes. This may be practical for her and enable her to begin to build on success, rather than having to deal with the frustration of attempting to study an impossible (for Susan) two hours in a row! The 15 minutes can be gradually expanded until Susan is studying in longer and longer time spans.

Susan's case is only one example of the application of information about student learning styles in the counseling situation. The counselor knows that whatever Susan is doing is not working. It doesn't help to tell her to study harder and longer at her desk. This suggestion has not worked in the past, as evidenced by Susan's unimproved grade-point average. Advice to do even more of something that has not been successful, such as studying three hours a night where two hours is not working, illustrates the "get a bigger hammer" approach to learning problems. It fails to respond to the individual differences that exist in each learner.

Knowledge of learning styles—the Dunns' model in this example—can provide guidelines for a systematic interview with the student and establish a useful basis for counseling. The interview allows for fine tuning the results of the instrument by letting the student personally verify those results. It helps remind the student that the information about style is neutral in terms of intelligence. The student also begins to discover that she knows how she prefers to learn and thus can begin taking responsibility for her own progress.

Students enjoy talking about how they like to learn. The problem is they are rarely asked! Essentially, the student is discovering that she does not have to learn like everybody else. Making the student more comfortable with a personal pattern of learning as well as responsible for becoming a more ef-

ficient learner can help to release some of the tension the student feels and
pave the way for grade improvement.

7. Curriculum

McCarthy's 4MAT System

Instruction begins when you, the teacher, learn from the learner, put yourself in his place so that you may understand what he learns and the way he understands it . . .

—Kierkegaard

Once upon a time in a town called Could It Happen, a young teacher was hired to come and start a new school. The school board asked this teacher to design the curriculum.

IF YOU WERE THE TEACHER IN THIS SCENARIO, WHAT WOULD YOU PRESENT TO THE school board? If we, as experienced educators, had an opportunity to design a curriculum from scratch, where would we start, what would we do, how would we build knowledge and skills, what would we consider important?

For most of us, such questions are answered by someone else, or at least we assume they are, and therefore we often don't take an active role in examining these issues. Let's put ourselves in the shoes of the young teacher in this scenario and explore some curriculum questions.

Curriculum Questions and Issues

What do we mean by curriculum? Do we mean the body of knowledge that we teach and expect students to learn? Do we mean the management of learning? Do we mean the applications of knowledge? Do we mean all of the above?

Curriculum issues truly do reflect diversity in thinking about schooling. For some educators, and for some of the general public, curriculum is a body of knowledge composed of facts, concepts, and skills that transmit societal and cultural values. These people put energy into defining and describing what students need to know to be well-educated people and good citizens. For some other educators and members of the public, curriculum should focus on the application of knowledge to develop the skills needed for a successful professional and personal life. These people ask what learners are going to do with the knowledge that they gain and how will they apply their learnings? Still other people believe curriculum should mean the skills needed to learn; it should be the process of learning to learn. For these people schools should teach processes of finding out, discovering, developing insights, organizing ideas, thinking analytically, and evaluating information. For these people curriculum should be designed to inspire a love of learning.

While certainly these perspectives on curriculum are not mutually exclusive, the emphasis on different beliefs is reflected in the variety of work on curriculum and in practical decisions about content and process. In a review of the writing about curriculum, Decker Walker (1980) concludes that curriculum is a diverse and varied area full of mixed opinions, values, purposes, and content. "Practically everything known to humanity is relevant, importantly so, to the resolution of some curriculum problem....Curriculum is clearly an iffy subject."

Another important and pervasive issue about curriculum is autonomy and control. Who makes the decisions, and who shall be accountable to whom? Should the federal government be involved in setting national directions by deciding, for example, that there should be more emphasis on science education in the elementary grades or foreign language skills among high school students or computer literacy at all ages? Should a local community have the final decision about which books should be in the school library, which topics children study in social studies classes, and the number of years of foreign language study are required for graduation?

Should professional educators, administrators, and teachers have the most active role in the decision-making process? Should a local school staff identify and decide upon the knowledge, skills, and process that will be emphasized in their building? Should students be permitted, or even encouraged, to have a say in what they learn? What role should the parents of students have in deciding what their children will learn?

Other pervasive issues in curriculum concern its organization and management. To what extent is the knowledge, the concepts, and the skills organized in a linear building-block fashion? To what extent are themes and relationships utilized to give meaning and context to learning? How much does a person need to know about something? Should a topic be studied in depth, or is it better for learners to survey an area in order to be well informed and knowledgeable about a variety of things?

Should curriculum be organized with careful attention to child development? Are students able to learn certain skills and information better at certain ages?

These questions and others are important and their answers not at all straightforward or simple. Responses to these questions guide the everyday practices in our schools, yet they are questions seldom asked by everyday practitioners. Much is taken for granted, and sometimes the buck is passed, often to the textbook publishers. If you had the opportunity that the young teacher above has, what would you do? And for our purposes in this book, how can the notion of individual styles guide us in some of these decisions?

To discuss these issues, this chapter focuses on the work of Bernice McCarthy and the 4MAT System of learning styles. Once again the reader is reminded that McCarthy's work is only one example of a way to address style and curriculum.

The 4MAT System—Bernice McCarthy

Bernice McCarthy is an experienced educator. She's taught various grade levels and has been a counselor and a teacher educator. Her own practical experience that students learn in different ways led her to do research on learning differences.

In 1979 she received a grant from the MacDonald Corporation to bring together several of the leading researchers in learning styles and brain functioning. From the exchange of ideas among these experts she developed her own approach to defining and explaining individual differences in learning. She synthesized a variety of learning style models but settled on the work of David Kolb as an umbrella descriptor of the learning process and the different ways people learn.

In the early 1970s, Kolb, a management expert from Case Western Reserve University, developed an experiential learning model. He identified two major dimensions of learning, perception, and processing, and said that learning results from the way people perceive and then process what has been perceived. He described two opposite kinds of perception. At one extreme are people who perceive through concrete experience, and at the other extreme are people who perceive through abstract conceptualization.

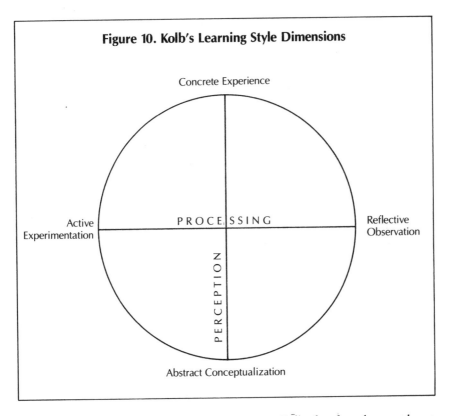

Figure 10. Kolb's Learning Style Dimensions

Concrete Experience

Active Experimentation

PROCESSING

Reflective Observation

PERCEPTION

Abstract Conceptualization

As he explored differences in processing, Kolb also found examples at opposite ends of a continuum. Some people process through active experimentation, while others process through reflective observation. The juxtaposition of the two ways of perceiving and the two ways of processing led Kolb to describe a four-quadrant model of learning styles (see Figure 10).

Focusing on Kolb's work and integrating the work of other learning style researchers, McCarthy described four types of learners. In Kolb's upper- right-hand quadrant, Type One learners are those who perceive through concrete experience and process through reflective observation. The second quadrant, called Type Two learners, are those who perceive through abstract conceptualization and process through reflective observation. In Quadrant III are the Type Three learners, those who perceive through abstract conceptualization and process through active experimentation. In Quadrant IV are the Type Four learners, who perceive through concrete experience and process through active experimentation. Each of these learners, because of individual differences in perception and processing, develops a unique pattern to learning.

Another area of study that fascinated McCarthy, and which she explored further in the conference mentioned above, was research on brain functioning. She was particularly interested in studies of hemisphericity and the findings that the right hemisphere and the left hemisphere specialize in certain kinds of tasks. This work led McCarthy to look carefully at each of her four types of learners and to explore how the right and left hemisphere would function for these unique learning styles. The final result was the imposing of the right and left specialization on each of the four learning styles, which she calls the 4MAT System (see Figure 11).

Type One learners perceive in a concrete sensing/feeling way and process in a reflective/watching way. Their right hemisphere searches for personal meaning through an experience, and the left hemisphere seeks to un-

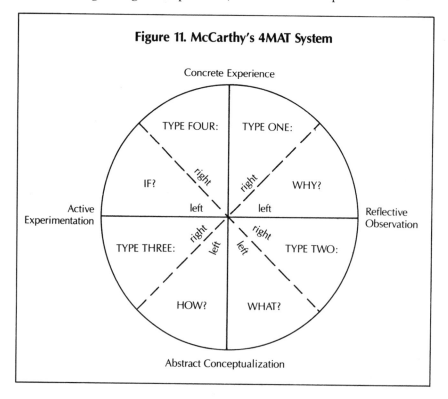

Figure 11. McCarthy's 4MAT System

derstand the experiencing by analyzing it. In the effort to find personal meaning, they often ask "Why?" Type One learners must think about what they personally value and care about; they must understand how learning will affect them and how it relates to their beliefs, feelings, and opinions. These learners seek a reason for learning and knowing something.

Type Two learners perceive in an abstract and thinking way and again process in a reflective and watching way. For them the most important question is "What?" Their right hemisphere seeks to integrate experience with what they know and to clarify their need for more knowledge, while their left hemisphere seeks that new knowledge. Type Two learners want to get accurate information. They want to deal with facts and right answers and be able to develop concepts and theories in an organized system. They care about exactness and detail and have a tremendous respect for authority and expertise. For these learners the important thing about learning is identifying what can be known and seeking knowledge carefully and fully.

Type Three learners also perceive by thinking and abstracting but they process by actively trying out and doing. For these learners, the most important question is "How does it work?" Their right hemisphere looks for an individual application and use of the learning, while their left hemisphere looks for more general "What have other people done?" examples. These learners want to try something, they want to practice, they want to be doing. It is this act of involvement that helps them to develop clear understandings and to test out information in the real world. They seek to make things useful, and they value things that are practical and have a concrete purpose. They care about the general application of knowledge and about how they personally are going to use what they are learning.

Finally, Type Four learners perceive through concrete sensing and feeling and process by doing. These learners ask the question "If?" Their right hemisphere seeks to develop extensions of their learning, and the left hemisphere seeks to analyze the learning for relevance and significance. Type Four learners want to see relationships and connections between things; they want to be inspired to do things that are really important in life. They seek to inspire other people and are often catalysts who make others excited about the learning process. They seek to synthesize skills and knowledge and personal meaning into something that creates a new experience for themselves and others. These learners understand and accept complexity.

McCarthy's 4MAT model describes the learning process as a natural sequence from the personal interests of Type One learners to the "If" questions of Type Four learners. McCarthy believes that all learners, and all learning experiences, should start with Quadrant I.

The 4MAT system moves throughout the learning cycle *in sequence,* teaching in all four modes and incorporating the four combinations of characteristics. The sequence is a natural learning progression that starts with the teacher answering—in sequence—the questions that appeal to each major learning style (1985:62, italics in original).

At first, personal meaning and motivation should be set for what is to follow. The next step should be acquisition of the new knowledge and concepts, followed by practical application. The final step is the more complex synthesis and extension. Thus, for McCarthy, every learning experience should begin at Quadrant I and follow through the cycle to its natural conclusion in Quadrant IV.

Using this sequence, she believes that each learning style will have an opportunity to shine part of the time. All learners will be able to develop their own natural abilities when they are working in their own strongest learning style area. At the same time they will develop other abilities necessary to be good learners by working in other quadrants. "Growth means going around the circle, honoring the processes and attributes of all four quadrants" (1985:63).

McCarthy emphasizes that what ordinarily happens in most schools is a very limited part of the eight-step process, concentrating primarily on the left quadrant for the Type Two learners and left quadrant for the Type Three learners. In other words, most schools deal with knowledge acquisition and general application. Therefore, utilizing the 4MAT System brings much more depth to a learning experience.

To illustrate how her model works, McCarthy has developed a number of lessons at all levels from kindergarten through college in which she shows that any content or process can be taught using her sequential eight-step system. To follow her lesson model a teacher would begin in Quadrant I by creating an experience and then a way for students to analyze the experience personally. Then step 3, now in Quadrant II, integrates the experience and continues to analyze in a more conceptual way, while step 4 actually develops new concepts. Continuing to Quadrant III, step 5 practices with what is given, and step 6 makes personal practical application. Finally, in Quadrant IV, step 7 synthesizes by looking for something relevant and original, and step 8 seeks to apply more complex experiences.

When teachers are trained in this eight-step lesson model, they experience greater or lesser ease with different steps in the process because of their own learning styles. It is easier, for example, for a Quadrant I style teacher to develop activities that create personal meaning and experience. At the same time it is easier for a Quadrant IV teacher to develop experiences that extend into the realm of new ideas and relationships. Quadrant II and Quadrant III teachers are helped by commercial curriculums and texts that particularly address left-mode experiences for acquisition of knowledge and the general practice of skills.

McCarthy (1980) has written several books to illustrate her model. The first, *The 4MAT System: Teaching to Learning Styles with Right/Left Mode Techniques,* is a general description and an overview of her model that includes sample lessons. In 1983 she and Susan Leflar edited a book called *4MAT in Action: Creative Lesson Plans for Teaching to Learning Styles with Right/Left Mode Technique.* This is a collection of lessons illustrating how the 4MAT System would work, with examples from primary grades to postsecondary schools and in diverse subject areas such as language arts, social studies, mathematics, and law. In 1985, with Bob Samples and Bill Hammond, she published *4MAT and Science: Toward Wholeness in Science Education.* This book illustrates how the 4MAT System would be exemplified in a total science program and also how specific science lessons can be taught through the 4MAT plan. All of these resource materials follow the same basic theme and description of the four- quadrant learners, and all emphasize a need for the sequential progress of learners through the eight-step learning experience.

For an assessment of an individual's learning style strengths, McCarthy uses David Kolb's Learning Style Inventory (1976). It presents groups of four words that are to be ranked. Numerical scores are computed for each of the four dimensions, and then the differences in scores on the perceptual and processing dimensions are calculated and plotted on a graph. Thus, a visual picture of one's placement in a particular learning quadrant is obtained. Kolb calls Type One learners "Divergers," Type Two learners "Assimilators," Type Three learners "Convergers," and Type Four learners "Accommodators."

Curriculum with Style

What would happen in a school that built curriculum based on knowledge of individual differences? In such a school, complex issues of content, purpose, control, and management would be addressed regularly.

When people in this school decided what was important to learn, they would consider the variety of opinions and beliefs of people with different styles. According to McCarthy's model, for example, it would be important that curriculum have personal meaning, that it answer the question "Why?" It would also be important that curriculum develop new knowledge based on accurate information to answer the question "What?"; be practical and deal with reality and personal application so that for each learner it answered the question "How?"; and be innovative, inspiring, and create new possibilities so that it would answer the question "If?"

A school that was building curriculum based on this comprehensive definition of learning would look at the content, the skills, and the attitudes it wanted students to develop in order to be sure that all aspects of each area were considered.

By the same token the question of who makes curriculum decisions could also be looked at through the 4MAT System. It will be important to think about why the decision is being made and therefore to consider who is in the position to answer "Why?" Also important would be defining what knowledge is important and recognizing that the varied interests of learners need to be considered. Those who care about the practical applications of learning—those who are eventually going to employ the students—also need to be involved in the decision. Finally, we must include those who seek a sense of purpose and inspiration from learning. They too would need to have a voice in curriculum decisions. Currently, one only needs to look at a few commercial texts to see that the designers are not representing these different perspectives.

How would curriculum in such a school be organized? If attention to individual differences were a primary concern, it would be clear that constant sequential organization would lead to an emphasis on limited aspects of knowledge and application, appealing to only a few learners. If a larger perspective were included, relationships, meanings, intuition, personal applications, hypothesis testing, observation, understanding, and appreciation would all need to be included in the organization. Therefore curriculum could be organized through themes, through the use of webs, and offer opportunities for in-depth study rather than constant surface coverage. Different organization frameworks would appeal to different learners.

Certainly it is clear that the issues surrounding decisions in curriculum are extremely complex. When we add to those issues the complexity of human diversity, we can understand why the easy road may be for many of us in education to pass the buck by letting the textbook companies and curriculum "experts" make the decisions for us. But, of course, we are making decisions daily in the many things we do regarding curriculum, whatever our professional roles. In a provocative essay on personal philosophy and curriculum, Arthur Foshay (1980) describes a number of metaphors about children and schooling which guide our actions in curriculum. Whether we acknowledge our biases openly or not, we all have some basic assumptions that are reflected in the daily big and small decisions we make about what's important to learn. We need to be aware of our own perspectives, which determine our behavior.

Students are learning something every moment at school, and much is in addition or contrary to planned or intended learnings. Curriculum issues are at the root of so many decisions, conscious or not, which affect learning. When we take up the challenge that understanding human diversity implies, we must continually seek to answer the question: What does each individual person want from schooling?

8. Instructional Methods

Modalities—Barbe and Swassing, and Dunn and Dunn

"Everything, men, animals, trees, stars, we are all one substance involved in the same terrible struggle. What struggle? ...Turning matter into spirit."

Zorba scratched his head [and said,] "I've got a thick skull boss, I don't grasp these things easily. Ah, if only you could dance all that you've just said, then I'd understand...Or if you could tell me all that in a story, boss."

—Nikos Kazantzakis
Zorba the Greek

Two roads diverged in a wood and I—
I took the one less travelled by,
And that has made all the difference.

Robert Frost
"The Road Not Taken"

Miss Tolbert is reading this well-known poem to her English class. When she finishes, she encourages the students to discuss what the poem means to them. Some of the children are very eager to share their ideas and experiences. Others, however, are drifting off; they seem distracted and begin to fidget and look at the clock. After a few more minutes, Miss Tolbert gives the children a homework assignment to memorize the poem. The next day some of the children enthusiastically want to recite the poem, while others are sullen, nervous, or disinterested.

In another school several miles away, Mr. Kerner is also using Frost's poem. Before he introduces the poem, he asks for some volunteers to act out a situation where a decision has to be made. After several such short scenarios followed by a brief discussion about making decisions, he passes out paper and crayons and asks the students to draw something about making a choice. He then reads the poem aloud to the class. For a second reading he uses an overhead transparency with the poem written on it and asks the class to follow along. Finally he asks the students how their skits and drawings might relate to the poem they have just been reading. A lively discussion ensues in which most of the class participates. In a little while he brings the discussion to a close and gives the assignment for the next day. Written on the board, it includes several choices, among which are memorizing the poem, illustrating it with a drawing, or acting out an example of its message. The next day the students return, anxious to share the projects they have chosen to do.

If we analyze the above situation in terms of style, we can see that in the first case the poem was presented in only one way and therefore appealed to a narrow range of students' styles. In the second case, because the poem was approached with a variety of techniques, it appealed to a much wider group of learners. It is likely that the overall objective of the lesson in each case was the same: that the students interpret the message of Robert Frost's poem. The difference in learning that occurs for the students, however, is directly related to *how* the material is presented.

This how, the method and the technique of instruction, can make a tremendous difference in the ultimate success of learning. We have all been in situations where, despite a positive attitude and strong motivation, we found it difficult to learn because of the method used to present the material. We realize that when given a choice of methods, we will select one that we know from experience works for us. As we observe people learning to use computers, for example, we notice some people use a hands-on approach while others appreciate a model and demonstration. Some computer neophytes purchase how-to books and carefully read manuals, while others will sign up for classes in order to learn computer skills with a teacher's direction. Even in physical skills, we exhibit the same variety in our approaches. Some of us learn to ski by getting on the skis and plunging down the slope, while others take lessons, watching carefully as the instructor demonstrates.

It is sometimes astonishing to see how improved our understanding can be when something is expressed in a different way. "Can you show me what you're talking about?" some of us will say when we're trying to visualize an idea. "Please tell me what I'm looking at," some of us will say when we want someone to explain a diagram or picture. "Let me try it myself," others of us will plead when we want to see if we understand. Each case represents an attempt to understand something *in the way* that makes most sense.

Experienced teachers know through common sense and from work with many different learners that children learn in different ways. This obviously leads teachers to try different techniques and methods. Knowledge of learning styles can make this effort to use diverse methods more systematic and more thorough.

In this section we will discuss the differences in modality strengths and preferences among learners as a basis for describing the importance of variety in instructional techniques and methods. Once again, focusing on the modality concept and relating it to methods is only one example of applying a styles model to an educational situation.

Modalities—Walter Barbe and Raymond Swassing; Rita Dunn and Kenneth Dunn

Modalities generally refer to the sensory channels through which we receive and give messages. A number of researchers have identified modality areas as examples of differences in style. Much of Maria Montessori's work was built on an understanding that children needed visual, auditory, tactile, and kinesthetic involvement in learning. More recently, different modality preferences and strengths have been identified and studied to help us understand children's and adults' styles. Rita and Kenneth Dunn include modality in their comprehensive battery of the elements that affect learning. (Chapter 6 discusses their model.)

Their colleague, Marie Carbo (1981), has included the modality area in her assessment of students' reading styles. And Walter Barbe, Raymond Swassing, and Michael Milone of The Ohio State University have focused on the modality differences in their definition of learning styles. "A modality is any of the sensory channels through which an individual receives and retains information. ...[S]ensation, perception and memory constitute what we are calling modality" (Barbe and Swassing, 1979:1). The auditory, visual, and kinesthetic/tactile modalities are identified as the most important sensory channels for education.

Auditory learners use their voices and their ears as the primary mode for learning. They remember what they hear and what they themselves express verbally. When something is hard to understand, they want to talk it through. When they're excited and enthusiastic about learning, they want to verbally express their response. And when an assignment is given orally, they will remember it without writing it down. These learners love class discussion, they grow by working and talking with others, and they appreciate a teacher taking time to explain something to them. They are also easily distracted by sound because they attend to all of the noises around them, but ironically they will often interrupt a quiet moment by talking because they find the silence itself disturbing.

When these students read, they often vocalize the words, sometimes mumbling, sometimes moving their lips. When they want to remember something, they will say it aloud, sometimes several times, because the oral repetition will implant it in their minds. When they tell you something, they assume you will remember it. When a teacher asks them to work quietly at their desks for an extended period of time or their parents ask them to study in a quiet room, these requests are difficult tasks. For some auditory learners, their abilities serve them well in learning music, foreign languages, and in other areas that depend on good auditory discrimination.

Some learners find their visual modality is much stronger in helping them understand and remember new concepts and skills. They want to actually see the words written down, a picture of something being described, a timeline to remember events in history, the assignment written on the board. These learners will be very attuned to all of the physical things in the classroom and will appreciate a pleasant and orderly physical environment. They will often carefully organize their own materials and will decorate their work spaces. As young children they want to see the pictures in the storybooks, and when they get older the same desire remains as they seek out illustrations, diagrams, and charts to help them understand and remember information. They appreciate being able to follow what a teacher is presenting with material written on an overhead transparency or in a handout. They review and study material by reading over their notes and by recopying and reorganizing in outline form.

Some learners find that they prefer, and actually learn better, when they touch and are physically involved in what they are studying. These learners want to act out a situation, to make a product, to do a project, and in general to be busy with their learning. As young children, they want to build and to handle materials constantly, and this desire stays with them as they elect shop and home economics in high school. They find that when they physically do something, they understand it and they remember it. As they get older, many of them take lots of notes to keep their hands busy, but they may never re-read the notes. They learn to use the computer by actually trying it, experimenting, and practicing. They learn concepts in social studies by simulating experiences in the classroom. They become interested in poetry by becoming physically involved in the thoughts expressed. Many of these learners want to be as active as possible during the learning experience. They express their enthusiasm by jumping up and getting excited when something is going well. And when asked to sit still for long periods, they fidget and are often labeled as behavior problems.

These different preferences and strengths in modality areas are familiar to all of us in education. We also know that many successful learners are able to function in more than one modality. The ability to bring a multimodal approach to a learning situation has tremendous payoff throughout the years of schooling. In terms of achievement, students with mixed modality strengths often have a better chance of success than do those with a single modality strength, because they can process information in whatever way it is presented.

In addition, many successful students have learned from experience to use their modality strengths to transfer learnings from the weaker areas. For example, as an aid to memory, strong visual learners typically will write down something presented in an auditory way. Unfortunately, many young learners do not have this transfer ability, and also in every classroom there are students who have strengths in only one sensory area.

Throughout this discussion the words "strength" and "preference" have been used together or interchangeably. Some researchers believe that modality sensitivity is a preference—something a person expresses a desire for. Others believe modality channels are strengths, which when used produce more success. This difference between preference and strength is illustrated in the variety of the instrumentation used to assess modality style. The Dunn, Dunn and Price Learning-Style Inventory described in Chapter 6, with its self-report questions, measures a student's preference for using one or more modalities.

The Swassing-Barbe Modality Index, on the other hand, tests modality strength. A student (from toddler through adult) is asked to use plastic shapes to repeat a given pattern. The patterns are presented sequentially in the oral, visual, then kinesthetic/tactile modalities, and a score representing successful repetition of the pattern is totaled for each of the modality areas. The actual numerical score is less important than the relationship of the three modality subscores. One would expect adults to repeat a higher number of patterns successfully. The relationship among one individual's scores describes the modality profile with its particular strengths or deficits. For example, 47 percent auditory, 28 percent visual, and 27 percent kinesthetic would show strong auditory strength.

Since a number of people have studied the modality area, research on various questions sometimes yields conflicting results. One area of disagreement revolves around the percentage of each modality style in the population as a whole and particularly in school-age populations. Barbe and Milone (1981) find that "Primary grade children are more auditory than visual, and are least well-developed kinesthetically" (p. 378). But Marie Carbo (1982) believes that most young readers approach reading through use of their "tactual/kinesthetic/visual skills—their auditory abilities are usually not well developed until fifth or sixth grade" (p. 43).

Another unresolved question is the relationship of modality perception, discrimination, and memory. Is it possible that a learner may have a very strong auditory memory but rather weak auditory discrimination? These issues and others reveal that while, on the surface, the study of modality style may seem relatively straightforward, further inquiry reveals the complexities in this model.

The modality area seems to be the best-known of differences in learning style among educators. For a number of years people in special education have been responding to modality differences in diagnostic and prescriptive work with students who have learning disabilities. A number of textbook companies are acknowledging modality differences by suggesting different ways for teachers to present, review, and evaluate the concepts and the skills presented in their materials. These beginning efforts are encouraging and exciting, and we hope they will grow within the next few years.

In Style with Instructional Methods

In a school that seriously attends to differences in learning styles by providing different instructional techniques and methods, the modality concepts can help assure that students have an opportunity to hear, to see, and to do each time a new concept is presented and reinforced. Teachers carefully evaluate their individual lessons to be sure students with different modality strengths find a way to understand the concepts. "Let me tell you," "Let me show you," "Let's do it," become standard comments in each classroom. When a child says, "I don't understand," the teacher attempts to explain the material in a different way than it was originally presented.

In a school that uses concepts of learning styles to encourage variety in teaching techniques, each staff member works to expand his or her own repertoire of methods, because

[W]e teach as we learn best, not as we were taught. [Teachers] tend to project their own modality strengths into their selection of materials, teaching strategies and procedures, and methods of reinforcement (Barbe and Swassing, 1979:14).

Teachers would examine this tendency to present material according to their own style and would seek to augment the presentation in ways that would meet the needs of a variety of students. The strong auditory teacher, for example, would recognize the tendency to explain new concepts and skills verbally and strive to bring more visual examples to the curriculum, and create more ways for the students to be physically involved in learning.

The strong visual teacher would realize the tendency to emphasize the neat presentation of work and to focus on a visual product such as a worksheet. Such teachers would strive to explain lessons verbally, even when it means repeating what is already written. These teachers would also strive to be patient with students who do not have a natural sense of visual order. The strong kinesthetic teacher would understand that not all children are excited by projects and products and would realize that the desire to have all students involved in their learning must include participation by reading and talking, as well as doing.

At the same time, a teacher would focus directly on the needs of the students, especially those who are having a more difficult time learning. Instead of just presenting the lesson in the same way louder and slower, teachers can "provide supplemental instruction, either individually or in small groups, that is consistent with the modality strengths of the children involved" (Milone, 1980, p.xiii). By working through the students' strongest learning modality, the teacher can then encourage the students to develop strategies to transfer material from weaker modalities.

Let's look at a spelling program in a classroom as a specific example. A teacher attending to diversity in students' styles would be sure that new spelling words were presented orally, visually, and through action. Students would be encouraged to study the words in ways that took advantage of their own modality strength. Tapes would be available for the auditory learner, written lists for the visual learner, and large markers, flash cards, and letter dice for the kinesthetic learner. When it was time for the test, students could be given a choice in the way they might take the test, or the teacher might vary the method of giving the test from week to week.

The importance of utilizing a variety of teaching methods is certainly not a new idea in education. Understanding differences in style can help strengthen a teacher's commitment to use diverse methods and bring a systematic approach to this effort.

PART III

USING STYLE

Figure 12. Making Use of Style

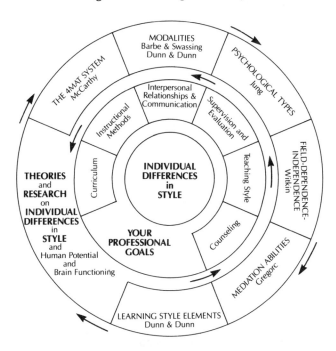

Making use of style concepts implies clarifying one's own beliefs about individual differences and identifying professional goals. Application then requires knowledge of theories and research on individual differences (personal style, human potential, and brain functioning). As the wheel is rotated, beliefs, goals, and theories and research are brought together to guide implementation.

9. Thinking About Style

Without an understanding of the unique meanings existing for the individual, the problems of helping him effectively are almost insurmountable.

—Arthur Combs
Helping Relationships

HOW DO CONCEPTS OF STYLE INFLUENCE OUR CURRENT PRACTICES OF SCHOOLING? In *The Third Wave,* futurist Alvin Toffler (1981) says that every civilization is guided by a hidden code that runs through all its activities. He points out that our society is most familiar with the principle of "standardization." In education, standardization is a common notion:

...to prepare youth for the job market, educators designed standardized curricula. Men like Binet and Terman devised standardized intelligence tests. School grading policies, admissions procedures, and accreditation rules were similarly standardized (pp. 47-48).

Closely related to standardization is another principle that Toffler calls "synchronization":

Pupils were conditioned to arrive at school when the bell rang, so that later on they would arrive reliably at the factory or office when the whistle blew....Children began and ended the school year at uniform times (p. 52).

Acceptance of the principles of standardization and synchronization logically leads educators to search for a standard model of schooling that will serve the needs of all students. The search extends to the identification of a best method for teaching all students. In the past decade these best methods have ranged from computer-assisted instruction to integrated curriculum and individualized programs. Each of these methods does prove effective with some students but produces little or no success with others. Standardized programs will achieve some measure of effectiveness, but if one accepts the fundamental existence of personality style, then the best that could be hoped for with any standardized program is limited success.

Both standardization and synchronization as they currently exist in the educational system stem from the fact that our current system developed within a highly industrialized society. Schools do exist within society, and the impact of society cannot be ignored. But our society has changed, and education must follow suit.

Style As An Approach to Education

Theories of style have the power for changing the status quo by focusing educational decisions on the individual person. Much of schooling is designed to "cover" material. Knowledge of style puts the focus on the meaning that the individual gleans from the material. Evolution toward this concept would involve teachers and students in a dynamic system of education that would have acceptance of individual differences as its base.

This framework will not lead to new models or programs to replace old ones. It is a fundamental change in attitude. Current models and programs will be retained when and as they are appropriate. Understanding of the needs of the individual will be the guideline. This attitude will bring frustration to those who seek a standard answer to questions of learning. But many educators already know, as Mackenzie (1983) reports in his review of effective schools research:

In the buzzing complexity of a school environment, imprecise answers may be precisely the kind to be sought. When a formula gives the appearance of great precision, it is almost surely going to be wrong (p. 13).

An Educator's Philosophy and Experience

Whether it is clearly articulated or not, every educator operates from a particular philosophical stance regarding the process of education. If personal philosophy does not value individual differences, the research and data on styles will not have meaning for an administrator or teacher. A recognition of individual differences must be based to an educator's philosophy if theories of style are to be used to approach learning and teaching.

Educators also bring practical experience to their jobs, and they should draw upon that experience as they seek to apply research on styles. In most instances an experienced teacher has discovered certain methods that work effectively in the classroom. To implement concepts of styles, a teacher need not necessarily be asked to give up these methods or even to change them drastically. Use of knowledge of styles should supplement what the teacher already knows and is already using.

As you reflect on the information about style presented in previous chapters, you are undoubtedly giving the theories personal meaning. This interpretation, formed from both your personal philosophy and experience, provides a framework for your decisions on how to use the theories of style. Bringing together your personal framework with the theories of style to form an approach to education can be explored philosophically by comparing the process to existential psychology.

Existential Psychology

Existential psychology has its roots in the work of the Danish philosopher Soren Kierkegaard and the German philosopher Friedrich Nietzsche. Rollo May (1958) builds on their work to express his thoughts about the existence of the person:

The term "existence," coming from the root *ex-sistere,* means literally to *stand out,* to *emerge.* This accurately indicates [an attempt] to portray the human being not as a collection of static substances or mechanisms or patterns but rather as emerging and becoming, that is to say, as existing. For no matter how interesting or theoretically true is the fact that I am composed of such and such chemicals or act by such and such mechanisms or patterns, the crucial question always is that I happen to exist at this given moment in time and space, and my problem is how I am to be aware of that fact and what I shall do about it (May, 1958:12, italics in the original).

By placing the emphasis on the person's existence, existential psychologists are able to speak about the person in a specific way.

The term the existential therapists use for the distinctive character of human existence is *Dasein.* . . Composed of *sein* (being) plus *da* (there), *Dasein* indicates that man is the being who *is there* and implies also that he *has* a "there" in the sense that he can know he is there and can take a stand with reference to that fact (May, 1958:41, italics in the original).

In his book *Existential Psychotherapy,* the psychoanalyst Irvin Yalom expands on the preceding notion when he states that

Dasein is at once the meaning giver and the known. Each *dasein* therefore constitutes its own world; to study all beings with some standard instrument as though they inhabited the same objective world is to introduce monumental error into one's observations (Yalom, 1980:23, italics in the original).

The existential psychologist recognizes the person as *dasein,* and therefore in "being there" that person is responsible for taking a stance toward the world, a world which is not the same to each individual. Recognition of this uniqueness characterizes the existential position regarding therapy. Existential psychology

... is not a system of therapy but an *attitude toward therapy.* Though it has led to many advances of technique, it is not a set of new techniques in itself but a concern with the understanding of the structure of the human being and his experience that must underlie all techniques (May, 1969:15, our italics).

Thus the existential movement in psychology "does not purport to found a new school as over against other schools" (May, 1958:7). It is a call to recognize that the client is unique regardless of the therapeutic method being used.

While the above discussion is no more than a brief reference to existential psychology, it is intended to illustrate ways that the existential attitude can be applied to a focus on styles in the field of education.

Existential Education

Yalom's statement quoted above, that "to study all beings with some standard instrument as though they inhabited the same objective world is to introduce monumental error into one's observations," is useful as one reflects that a similar monumental error would be committed in teaching all beings "as though they inhabited the same objective world." Theories describing style exist to prevent this error. All of the different theories have in common two basic thrusts:

1. a recognition of a person's individuality; and
2. an attempt to provide the means to act upon that recognition.

Very few educators would blatantly state they do not recognize individual differences. Therefore it makes little sense to speak of a "learning styles teacher" as opposed to, for example, a traditional or an "open-concept teacher." In a sense every teacher is "existential" and "learning styles oriented" to the extent that he or she is an effective teacher. Thus many educators will find in the various theories of styles a systematizing of what they already know: that people are different in how they perceive, think, feel, and act. Consequently, all aspects of education must recognize these differences. An effective educator responds to differences whether the school setting is traditional, open, or alternative.

This fact should not oversimplify the complexities involved in teaching 20 to 35 individual students in a classroom at one time. Teaching involves hundreds of immediate "decisions that require artistry—a fine, swift, intuitive sense of situations" (Hunter, 1979:45). Styles can, however, provide some basis for the swift sense of a situation by helping the teacher to keep the focus on the individual.

In the classroom the teacher is also *dasein,* and the teaching process is a reciprocal relationship between teacher and learner.

> The interchange between a teacher and her pupils will be different every moment, and the teacher must be prepared to react to each child in terms of the unique question, idea, problem, and concern that he is expressing at that particular instant (Combs, and others, 1971, p. 5).

The teacher receives information necessary to refine the act of teaching and can alter that teaching based on feedback from the student. In similar fashion, the student receives feedback from the teacher and can adjust his or her learning. Both teacher and student are learning. The error of overemphasizing methods or programs leads to a focus on the method rather than on the person who makes meaning from the method. Approaching learning with styles in mind is something the teacher does in cooperation with the students and not as another program done to the student.

Gerald Kusler (1984), an educator who works with theories of style, says:

> Great chunks of the research support a simple dictum: *know* yourself; *know* your students, believe in what both can do. Because of cognitive and learning style work we can *know* ourselves and our students in a way that counts—as learners and thinkers (1984, p. 14, emphasis in original).

Educators must borrow from the existential psychologists the view that the concept of styles is an *attitude* or an *approach* that is brought to the education process. Theories of style do not provide a new set of techniques to constitute a standardized method of style; rather these theories provide an approach to methods already being used. This is not meant to rule out the fact that new practices or methods may emerge from a study of information about styles, but these should not be the primary focus in the implementation of an approach to education using style.

10. Some Issues and Applications

I desire that there be as many different persons in the world as possible; I would have each one be very careful to find out and preserve his own way.

—Henry David Thoreau

SINCE THE STUDY OF STYLE IS SO COMPLEX, THERE ARE A NUMBER OF UNRESOLVED issues that sometimes bring conflicting messages from the researchers. At the same time there are also a variety of options for using this information and these concepts. This chapter highlights some of the more important areas: origin, development, and change; culture and sex; neutrality, intelligence, and achievement; assessment of style; diverse approaches to style; and style in context of some current concerns.

Origin, Development, and Change

What forms our basic personality style? The answer seems to be that both nature and nurture play a part in the origin of style. Psychologists, especially, believe that we are born with the foundation of our style patterns.

Carl Jung (1927, in Wickes) discussed origin of type by referring to the unique personalities of each child in a family:

For all lovers of theory, the essential fact...is that the things which have the most powerful effect upon children do not come from the conscious state of the parents but from their unconscious background... Here as elsewhere in practical psychology we are constantly coming up against the experience that in a family of several children only one of them will react to the unconscious of the parents with a marked degree of identity, while the others show no such reaction. The specific constitution of the individual plays a part here that is practically decisive (pp. xix-xx).

Psychologist Frances Wickes (1927), working under Jung's guidance, wrote that "We must think of life as developing from within as well as from without...each [child] bears within himself the germ of his own individuality" (pp. 13-14). Recent researchers, such as Barbe and Swassing (1979), also recognize both nature and nurture: "...the definition we are proposing acknowledges the role of both heredity and the environment in shaping an individual's modality strengths "(p. 5).

Certainly experience does play an important part in who we are. One way to think about the balance of nature and nurture is to consider the aspects of the person that style describes. We previously identified differences in cognition, conceptualization, affect, and behavior. Certain of these traits are probably more affected by experience than others. One could argue that cognitive and conceptual characteristics are deep-rooted but that behavior can be more easily learned. As one reads different researchers' explanations for the roots of style, their reasoning often reflects their basic definition of style. Those who focus primarily on behavior are likely to attribute more importance to experience, for example.

A number of researchers discuss the importance of the development of style. Essentially their message is that both competence and self-esteem come from using natural stylistic traits. If I'm naturally inclined toward certain patterns of behavior, I will be at my best in these areas. If I get strokes for these behaviors, I will feel good about myself. With a strong sense of self, I am in a better position to learn behaviors natural to other styles. If, on the other hand, my own natural traits are not valued, they will not develop to their fullest and I may wonder "what's wrong with me?" One mother illustrated this dilemma in a workshop we conducted with a parent group when she shared a personal story:

Let me tell you about my son. He's always daydreaming, staring into space. It really worries me that he does nothing. Today, for example, he was staring out the window, so I timed him. Ten minutes! Then he turned to me and he said, 'Mom, the moon is banana-shaped.' Then he turned toward the window again; four more minutes. 'Mom, if the moon is banana-shaped, it can't be round.' Do you see what I mean? Why would he waste his time just looking out the window at the moon?

This mother went on to explain that while she values doing and action, learning about style helped her realize that her child obviously places a value on abstracting and imagining. She realizes that to fully develop his own style, this child will need to feel accepted and loved for what he does naturally and easily. If he feels this acceptance, he will then be open to his mother's emphasis on doing and action. In the ideal situation, this child could learn to value and use his strengths as well as to develop skills to approach life in other ways. On the other hand, if his mother does not value his intuition and abstraction, the child may come to question his own strengths. It is certainly easier for each of us to be flexible if our sense of self is clear and secure. A positive self-esteem opens us to growth and change.

Can we change our style? In a review of the Myers-Briggs research, Hoffman and Betkouski (1981) conclude that

... patterns of behavior—are deep in each person's psychological makeup. Lawrence's model refers to this behavior as being unchangeable as the stripes on a tiger. . . . Keirsey said it another way, "The unfolding rose may blossom to its fullest but will never be a sunflower "(p. 25).

In response to the same question in her summary review of research on styles, Claudia Cornett (1983) says, "Yes, but. . . ."

So while the learning style blueprint is initially based on inheritance and prenatal influences, a person's learning predisposition is subject to qualitative changes resulting from maturation and environmental stimuli. . . . Throughout life, all people are subject to changes *within a relatively stable overall style structure* (p. 12, our italics).

Since educators recognize that certain style traits are related to success in specific school tasks, the question of changing styles is very important. When a learner's style is dysfunctional for specific school tasks, who adapts—the learner or the school? This question, discussed in more detail further in the chapter, brings mixed responses from researchers, based to some extent on their beliefs about the feasibility of changing style. For now this question of change remains unresolved both philosophically and practically.

Culture and Sex

Is an individual's style related to culture? Is it related to sex?

Researchers who have examined these questions generally find that socialization plays a role in the development of style differences in people of various cultures and in both sexes. For example, the Myers-Briggs research (Lawrence, 1979/1982) has found that women are more likely to be on the feeling end of the thinking/feeling continuum while men tend to be close to the thinking end, with a 60 percent-40 percent differentiation both times. However, since we know that in our society women are generally expected to behave with more feeling-type characteristics and thus are reinforced for those behaviors, it is not surprising to find the sex differentiation. Another commonly held social stereotype, that boys are more kinesthetic than girls, was not substantiated, however, in Barbe's modality research (Barbe and Malone, 1984).

Culturally the same socialization is evident. Witkin's nonverbal field-embedded measures have been administered in many different cultures revealing significant relationships when a particular perceptual approach is a direct adaptation to the needs of the society. For example, studies with Witkin's model found that nomadic hunting and gathering societies tended to be relatively more field independent, an appropriate style for their life patterns (Witkin and Goodenough, 1981). A number of researchers, particularly Ramirez and Castaneda (1974), have described the tendency of Mexican-American children to behave in a more field-dependent way, and again characteristics of that style are valued by the culture.

It is probably fair to conclude that research does not currently offer substantial evidence that style is innately different for cultures or sexes, but certainly the knowledge of socialization of certain style characteristics should add more reasons for educators to be sensitive to the expectations and behaviors of cultures and sexes different from their own.

Neutrality, Intelligence, and Achievement

Is there a "best" style?

Throughout this book we've defined style as neutral. This implies that there is no better, best, good, or poor style. Most of the researchers discuss the potential positives and the potential negatives of various patterns of style:

... the field-dependence-independence dimension is bipolar with regard to level, in the sense that it does not have clear "high" and "low" ends. Its bipolarity makes the dimension value-neutral, in the sense that each pole has qualities that are adaptive in particular circumstances.... We thus see that field dependence and field independence are not inherently "good" or "bad" (Witkin and Goodenough, 1981, p. 59).

This fundamental notion is the very basis of valuing diversity, since viewing every style as having inherent qualities that can be potential strengths eliminates the temptation to judge a person's style solely against set criteria.

Fine, but are people with a certain style "smarter"? A number of researchers have studied the relationship between style and intelligence. They have found that some tasks in intelligence tests actually measure style. Barbe and Swassing (1979) feel that Binet and Simon's original measurements, which deal with "memorizing series of digits and matching patterns of beads, were primarily tests of modality strengths" (p. 33). Also the Wechsler Block Design, Object Assembly, and Picture Completion subtests, all of which require restructuring, have been shown in studies to favor a field-independent style (Witkin and Goodenough, 1981, p. 61).

After acknowledging the testing bias, however, the majority of researchers on style agree with Hoffman and Betkouski (1981), who concluded after a comprehensive review of type research that intelligence is independent from style. "Type theory indicates . . . differences are related to varying interests and not necessarily a superiority of ability of one type over another" (p. 18).

On the other hand, a number of research studies have found correlations between style and achievement in school. The conclusion seems to be that it pays off in school to have certain stylistic characteristics that are more consistently successful with school tasks.

As early as 1927, Jungian child psychologist Wickes reported:

Usually it is the thinking type of child who shows to best advantage in the school, for school is primarily the place of intellectual development, and thinking is the intellectual form of adaptation to reality (p. 120).

Recent reviews of the type literature have also shown that "Intuitives appear to have the greater potential for success in school from the beginning. Most classroom instruction is based on the use of symbols, an area in which intuitives show up well" (Hoffman and Betkouski, 1981, p. 18). This particular dichotomy between dominant-sensing and intuitive-type students was dramatically illustrated in an extensive research study in Florida conducted by the Governor's Task Force on Disruptive Youth. A sample of more than 500 adults who did not complete eighth grade showed that 99.6 percent were sensing types. The same study showed that of 671 finalists for National Merit Scholarships, 83 percent were intuitives (McCaulley and Natter, 1974, 1980, p. 128).

So a dilemma arises. If style is not directly related to intelligence, why are some styles more successful in school? Related to this question is evidence that success in professions, business, and industry is possible for people of all styles and seems to be a matter of the right style match to the requirements of the particular profession or job. It has been interesting to note, for example, that recent studies of productivity in industry emphasize the importance of people skills and intuition, which have not been visibly valued in Western industrialized societies. In their description of successful American companies in *In Search of Excellence,* authors Peters and Waterman (1982) focus on the importance of these approaches and patterns:

...we have to stop overdoing things on the rational side.... Our imaginative, symbolic right brain is at least as important as our rational, deductive left. We reason by stories at least as often as with good data. "Does it feel right?" counts for more than "Does it add up?" or "Can I prove it?" (pp. 54-55).

In education, too, we need to examine what qualities to emphasize and value. Are we giving all styles equal chances for success? Since research and experience do confirm the value of all styles, we should be teaching students, by our example, that whatever an individual's style, each person has the potential for success and satisfaction in school and beyond.

Assessment of Style

How do we know what a person's style is? When should we assess style? Who should assess style? How valid are assessment instruments?

There are basically five ways to assess style (Fig. 13, p. 82). The first is to use self-report instruments. This is the most common assessment technique available and includes the Gregorc Style Delineator, the Dunns' Learning Style Inventory, and the Myers-Briggs Type Indicator, all mentioned in previous chapters. Many similar assessments are available for use in education, business, and with other professions. These instruments ask a person to rank responses to some questions and/or words. They usually force a choice and are scored to show the person's style through the patterns of the responses made.

With self-report instruments, people give direct information about themselves and often feel very comfortable with the results. These instruments have a potential weakness, however, in that responses from some people reflect wishful thinking and mood rather than reality. Perhaps more important, Carl Jung (1921) is only one researcher who questions a person's self-knowledge: "In respect of one's own personality, one's judgment is as a rule extraordinarily clouded" (p. 3).

The second kind of assessment is a test of a particular skill or task. The Embedded Figures Test described in the chapter on Witkin's work and the

---

Figure 13. Ways to Assess Style*

INVENTORIES
Direct self-report:
- Learning Styles Inventory (LSI) (Dunn, Dunn and Price)
- Myers-Briggs Type Indicator (MBTI) (Myers-Briggs)
- Communicating Styles Survey (Mok)
Indirect self-report:
- Gregorc Style Delineator (Gregorc)
- Learning Style Inventory (Kolb, used by McCarthy)

TESTS
- Embedded Figures Test (Witkin)
- Swassing-Barbe Modality Index (Barbe and Swassing)

INTERVIEW
- Open-ended conversation
- With "Inventory" questions
- Writing one's own profile as a learner

OBSERVATION
- Checklists (Lawrence, Barbe and Swassing)
- Anecdotal records

ANALYSIS OF PRODUCTS OF LEARNING
- Achievements
- Errors (e.g., reading miscue-analysis)

*All instruments cited are listed in the references.

Swassing-Barbe Modality Index are examples of this type of instrument. In a test assessment, a specific task has been shown to correlate with style characteristics, and the degree of success with the task indicates the style. A test assessment has the advantage of being objective, but it is limited to measurement of skill in a specific task, and extensions are inferred.

The third way to assess style is to ask a person directly. An interview may use questions from a self-report instrument or may be open-ended in its approach. With an interview one needs to be aware that both the interviewer and interviewee are affected by their own styles, so they will both bring their own perspectives to the conversation.

The fourth way to assess style is to observe a person at a task or in a particular situation. A number of researchers encourage teachers to observe students and have provided checklists to help systematize the process (Lawrence, 1982, and Barbe and Swassing, 1979). As with an interview assessment, the observation of another person will be colored by the observer's perception, and this interaction needs to be considered.

The fifth method of assessment is to look at the products of a person's behavior. Activities that are easy and consistently successful for an individual will give us indications of that person's pattern and approach. By the same token, the tasks and situations that are consistently difficult will give us information, too. Readers who retain accurate, detailed information but have a difficult time with inferences, for example, are indicating something about their style. One teacher we worked with used a miscue-analysis approach to assess the reading style of several students. The results were very dramatic and correlated strongly with several characteristics of style.

The authors of style-discerning instruments point out that no instrument is 100 percent valid for every person. Therefore they suggest diagnosis of styles through the use of more than one assessment technique. The authors of many self-report instruments, for example, encourage people to use interviews and observations in conjunction with their instruments.

When should we assess style? This question must be answered by identifying the purpose of a formal assessment. When teachers assess their own style, they can study their own patterns in order to understand and strengthen their approaches to teaching. A personal and careful assessment of the style of a learner who is at risk of failing could yield very valuable and helpful information.

But in the case of teachers responsible for a great number of students, the assessment of each student's style implies having plans to accommodate the individual differences they find. Administrators and teachers in this instance must be clear about the purpose of such an effort. Caution should be exercised in the widespread assessment of style, lest unrealistic expectations be set and frustrations result. One example of an appropriate school-wide assessment comes from one author's experience as a high school counselor. The style of each entering freshman was assessed and entered in the student's file. Teachers, parents, and students received the general results. When they asked specific questions or expressed concerns, the information on styles was applied. Teachers, parents, and students saw the information as a resource rather than an evaluation or a mandate for change.

Who should assess style? Although many of the instruments and tests can be administered without formal training, it would be naive to assume that anyone administering an instrument would be able to effectively use its results. People should have a depth and breadth of knowledge about style when they assess patterns of individuals or groups. Too often the first thing a person wants to do after an initial introduction to style is administer an assessment to others. Although this may provide interesting information, it doesn't always serve the ultimate purpose of respecting and responding to individual differences. If that purpose is not served, the assessment bears more relation to determining a person's zodiac sign than to providing clear, educationally useful data.

Assessment is often thought to be a necessary first step in application of concepts of style, but as we have illustrated previously, many accommodations to style can be made by a genuine acceptance of diversity without specifically labeling the diversity of each person. Consciously accommodating style through variety in curriculum and instructional methods is realistic and ultimately beneficial for many learners.

We also need to be aware that however well validated, each instrument to assess style is only as reliable as the purpose it is designed to serve. Assessments of cognitive processing infer behavior; personality instruments make generalizations about approaches to learning; behavior assessments are often situational. Since researchers focus their work on certain aspects of personality, and real people are multidimensional, it will not be surprising that any instrument will only give a partial picture.

Assessing style should be approached cautiously and with a clear purpose. The more one understands the many dimensions of style, the less hasty one is to make judgments and impose labels.

Diverse Approaches to Style

As the theories of style develop, both agreement and diversity emerge among the definitions, concepts, applications, and instrumentation. Each researcher creates a personal definition and uses specific vocabulary. The lack of unanimity can lead educational researchers to work on formulating a synergistic definition of styles by pulling together the various strands of thought to form something greater than the sum of the parts. Philosophers call this a paradigm. As defined by Kuhn (1970:viii), this paradigm would be "universally recognized [as providing] model problems and solutions to a community of practitioners" in the world of education.

At first glance the need for a synergistic model seems important—especially in view of the rapidity with which the data about styles have been accumulating. However, despite the temptation of creating one synergistic theory, this goal may be both premature and unnecessary.

The research on styles appears to be in what Kuhn (1970) calls the pre-paradigm period, a time in the research that "is regularly marked by frequent and deep debates over legitimate methods, problems, and standards of solution, though these serve rather to define schools than to produce agreement" (pp. 47-48). This stage is further "characterized by continual competition between a number of distinct views" (Kuhn, 1970:4).

A desire for a synergistic model of styles can once again lead educators to look for a program to standardize and synchronize education in the way discussed in Chapter 9. It is a contradiction to believe that any one definition of style or any particular instrument will be applicable to each individual. If the many models of style are viewed as providing a wealth of resources for schools rather than as a source of confusion, the problem of the practicing educator then becomes one of determining which theory will provide the needed approach for each particular circumstance. This decision does not lead to choosing the one right definition or model of styles but causes a thoughtful, comprehensive approach to be brought to the distinct and unique needs of each situation.

Style in Context

Since style describes process rather than product, it is a pervasive factor. In all our concerns in education we need to keep the individual differences of people in the forefront. Let's consider briefly some examples of style in relation to several current issues.

Parenting

Perhaps the most important people who need to understand the concept of individual style are parents. The ability to accept the unique personality of each child is tied to understanding the value of style differences. We assume all parents want the best for their children. But the best needs to be appropriate for the individual child in light of that child's natural approaches and personality. Parents may readily accept this concept intellectually but find it more difficult to put it into practice, as the mother's story about her intuitive son illustrated earlier in this chapter.

Since a child's self-esteem is directly tied to approval by parents, especially in the early years, an understanding of style differences can have far-reaching implications later in life. As a child matures, parents who understand the style patterns of each of their children will be more successful in helping them to manage school relationships and tasks—and eventually to make wise career choices and decisions. A booklet, *Where Did We Get This One? A Parents' Guide to Appreciating the Individual Personalities of Their Children* (Guild and Hand, 1985), is one resource for helping parents understand style.

Critical Thinking Skills

The emergence of our information-oriented society plus the fast pace of technological changes have renewed interest in critical and higher-level thinking. Responsible educators recognize that truly learned and educated people are good thinkers with the ability to analyze, synthesize, apply, and judge the value of their learning.

When we study the processes involved in critical thinking, we can put on our "style glasses" and see that natural perceptions and conceptual processes have a tremendous effect on the way people think. It is not difficult for some people to utilize personal reflection, values, and judgments in processing objective information. Some people naturally see the practical application of certain content. And some people readily analyze cause-and-effect relationships. But depending on our mind processes—our style—different aspects of thinking are easy or more or less difficult for different people. This is a challenging area that remains to be explored in more depth.

Computers

Will computers and their associated technology revolutionize the way we teach and learn? Certainly the impact of this technology on schools and at home offers tremendous potential for learning. Here, too, the concepts of style need to be considered. People approach the technology with different techniques, different strengths, and certainly different interests. They will find a variety of uses for the technology depending on their own needs, their experiences, and, of course, their styles. As people learn to use computers, they bring their own approach and learn more effectively if their style is accommodated. Some children and adults want to leap before they look, while others are hesitant to be involved with a computer until they feel that they understand its purpose and operations.

Also important is the opportunity that this technology offers to manage learning in ways that allow for more options. It is certainly possible that a computer program focusing on division of fractions, for example, could offer a variety of approaches to learning that concept. A student could select a certain approach, or a computer itself could make the selection based on the kinds of errors, problems, and questions that the student has with the initial presentation of the concept. Again, this is an important area for further study.

Multicultural Goals

While we have stated previously in this chapter that the relationship of culture and style is not entirely clear, the concepts of style have definite implications for multicultural goals in education. The active recognition of personal differences in style demands an effort to fully understand each individual. This focus extends to an understanding of each person's cultural roots and values. The acceptance of style and cultural values as fundamental strengths of each individual contributes to the development of self- esteem. When we direct our thinking toward a celebration of diversity, we value the cultural uniqueness of each person.

Another goal of multicultural education is respect for differences among people. The study of style can contribute directly to this goal by emphasizing the unique strengths of each person. As we seek to help every student and staff member recognize that it is the very differences among people that bring strength to our educational institutions, this recognition will carry over to attitudes toward society. The goals of multicultural education and style go hand in hand. It would be exciting to see these areas explored together in future studies and applications.

Excellence and Effectiveness

The recent focus on excellence and effectiveness in our schools has led us to identify certain common characteristics of successful schools. Does this then lead to the conclusion that there are better and best ways to meet the needs of all students, teachers, and parents? Perhaps at first glance, but when one carefully reads the research, it becomes clear the generalizations and conclusions are frameworks, and that the message of respect for individual diversity is constantly reiterated. In his extensive review of the effective schools research, Mackenzie (1983) agreed with Purkey and Smith's description of a school as a small culture. He finds:

In this environment, nothing works all the time. Almost anything that makes sense will work more often than not, if it is implemented with enough self-critical optimism and zest. Some things work more often than others, but hardly anything works for everybody (p. 13).

Since excellence and effectiveness are aims of every educator, there is no question that we profit from studies of what works. But to define excellence without respecting and responding to the individual differences of learners, staff, and parents is shallow indeed.

Accommodating Style

How do we accommodate differences in style? Do the schools and educational institutions need to adapt to the diverse styles of the people who work and study there, or do the people who come to the institutions need to meet the demands of the structure and organization? In an individual teaching-and-learning situation, does the teacher adapt to the student or the student to the teacher? Do parents adapt to the styles of each of their children, or do the children adapt to the styles of the parents?

One could argue that with the large numbers of people who work in schools, uniform and standard approaches have to be prescribed. The issue is perhaps deciding when uniformity and standard requirements are necessary. It is a matter of emphasis and of direction. Is education moving toward conformity or toward respect for individual differences? When we decide on a uniform curriculum program, for example, we are definitely deciding that the students must adapt their styles to the demands of this particular curriculum approach. When we require all teachers be evaluated in the same way, we are demanding that the teacher meet the style demands of that evaluation process.

Researchers on style have different opinions about this issue. Some researchers believe that schools and teachers must adapt. Others believe that learners must be given the skills required for success in school, and still others advocate a little bit of each. The Dunns (1975), for instance, urge us to meet the needs of the individual learners as often and as frequently as possible. Gregorc (1982) and Witkin (1977), on the other hand, encourage a direct accommodation of style at various times and a conscious mismatch at other times in order to help people to stretch themselves.

Charles Letteri (1982) of the University of Vermont argues for training students in the skills needed to meet the demands of school. His research has found that certain cognitive characteristics are directly related to academic achievement. If a student has a specific cognitive profile, Letteri predicts success; an opposite profile can indicate failure. By using seven bipolar dimensions, his model considers the relationships among style variables and proposes that specific combinations of style characteristics are red flags for academic problems. For example, a student who is "field-dependent," "impulsive," a "leveler," and has a "low tolerance for ambiguity" will consistently test lower academically than a student with opposite bipolar characteristics. Letteri argues that learners can and should be trained to develop success-oriented cognitive skills. Other researchers question the practicality and desirability of such effort and point out that long-term achievement, success, and effect on self- esteem are still not known.

In many cases knowledge of a learner's style can lead us to develop a specific approach to more efficiently and effectively teach that learner. A diagnostic-prescriptive approach to teaching can lead to success for students who have previously experienced failure. Effective diagnostic-prescriptive teaching involves careful collection of diagnostic information using appropriate assessment instruments, substantiated by observation and interaction with the person being assessed. It also assumes a knowledge of appropriate prescriptive teaching responses and materials so that the learner's dominant style can be used. This kind of careful and thoughtful process is probably most appropriate when a teacher is responsible for only a small group of learners. Many special education teachers successfully develop specific programs to meet the unique needs of each student. Using research on styles to design diagnostic-prescriptive teaching programs is a sensitive area with more challenge than initially apparent since it involves the interaction of human nature and intelligence with the concepts, content, and skills being taught in schools. It must be done carefully.

In addition, review of studies on the effects of matching "conclude that style matching can be strongly supported for affective reasons, but overall style matching produces inconsistent achievement outcomes" (Cornett, 1983, p. 41). Again this is a complex and unresolved area needing further study.

Knowing that any group of people in education—administrators, teachers, parents, students—are going to have diverse styles leads to the conclusion that programs, structures, and expectations must offer variety. In some cases it may not not be as important to know exactly the style of each person we interact with as it is to act upon the assumption that in any group of people a diversity of styles will be represented.

Therefore in all decisions, in all organizational structures, in all interactions, and in all methods of instruction, it is important to have variety. Whenever possible, the people involved should be given optional approaches to particular tasks.

Although using variety and diagnostic-prescriptive approaches in teaching concepts and skills is certainly not a new idea to teachers, most educators would agree that we have a long way to go to really provide for diversity in learners' styles. There is seldom only one way to do or say something, or to learn. It is this understanding that will encourage all of us to value variety in style in our particular roles in education. Teachers and administrators who understand these concepts consciously attempt to respond to the diversity regularly encountered in schools.

11. Implementing Style

. . . Irvin Feld had found that their talents complemented each other. Kenneth, for example, takes particular interest in the beginning of a concept. He has a gift for picturing in his mind how the show will look on opening night even before the first rehearsal has been held. Irvin Feld, on the other hand, looks forward to the final rehearsals—when a detail can be added, a refinement made, that will make the highlights of the show really sparkle—the way a jeweler polishes the facets of a diamond. This combination of the son who likes to look at the big picture and the father who pays attention to the tiniest detail, gives a depth to their productions that is part of the Feld Approach.

—Souvenir Program
Ringling Brothers and Barnum & Bailey Circus

WHAT SHOULD EDUCATORS DO TO ACCOMMODATE THE DIVERSITY OF STYLES adults and students bring to schools? Chapters 3 through 8 illustrate specific ideas for using concepts and research on style in communication and interpersonal relationships, supervision and evaluation, counseling, teaching style, curriculum, and instructional methods. This chapter builds on those illustrations by discussing staff development efforts that are directed toward applying concepts of styles.

All competent educators can identify a variety of ways they respect individual differences. Study of the formal research on styles can serve to strengthen their resolve as well as bring a more systematic plan to their efforts. It can also prod and challenge teachers and administrators who may be neglecting the active recognition of style differences in students or teachers. Since style differences are evident every day to educators, experienced teachers and administrators are able to develop numerous ways to accommodate style when they are encouraged and directed to make the effort. The way each educator puts these theories and concepts into action is, of course, a reflection of personal style. Here, too, choices must be respected, and diversity must be celebrated.

Some applications of research on style are very systematic and formal, beginning with the study of a particular model, and then developing and implementing specific strategies to respond to staff and student diversity. Other applications are more informal, perhaps subtle, with human diversity valued throughout the school in pervasive ways, though the word style may seldom be used.

In our workshops and classes over the past 15 years, administrators and teachers have found many creative ways to accommodate differences in style. Some have studied their own styles to understand the demands they make on those with whom they work and to identify areas of needed growth. Some have analyzed their standard curriculum programs in the context of styles and then reworked that curriculum to reach more learners. Some have taught students and parents about style, urging them to be aware of their own patterns and to develop ways to use strengths and compensate for weaknesses. One teacher's work with students is the basis for a booklet on study skills and style: *No Sweat! How To Use Your Learning Style To Be A Better Student* (Ulrich and Guild, 1985) is a practical, lively guide to style written to help students identify and use their strengths.

Some researchers believe that a serious effort to accommodate differences in style in education must result in a total restructuring of our schools. When diversity of style is accepted and acted upon, and we no longer search for the right or best answer to questions of content or process in education, we will always start with the individual and what is best for that person in that particular situation. This leads to a focus on the dynamic interaction among people, content, and process in the institutions of education. Their design and reality must reflect that interaction.

Staff Development with Style

Staff development efforts should elicit enthusiasm and excitement from teachers. They should offer opportunities for elementary teachers, high school teachers, administrators, parents, and other members of the school community to participate together in activities for their own professional and personal growth. They should encourage teachers who work next door to each other to share ideas and reinforce each other's strengths. We've seen the concept of style, used as an umbrella for a variety of efforts in staff development, produce all of the above positive results.

About Staff Development

The theories, concepts, and ideas that have been discussed in previous chapters give us some messages *about* staff development. Respect for individual differences and diversity implies staff development programs that give substantial decision-making power to staff. The people whose growth is the goal of improvement efforts should have a good deal of say over the process and content. When we believe that differences in style can contribute positively to schools, staff development efforts will be used to encourage individual personal growth. This concept implies an acceptance of different professional interests and needs based on individual style.

Since we have shown throughout the book that concepts of style relate to all aspects of the educational process, all staff development efforts should include attention to style. Those efforts to design, evaluate, or implement curriculum should include attention to individual differences. And efforts directed at developing specific instructional skills need to focus on the individual differences of teachers and students. Too often a school staff will have inservice training on computers, for example, on Tuesday, then a learning styles session on Thursday—and never the twain shall meet. No wonder teachers get frustrated!

Most important, formal and informal staff development efforts need to be reinforced every day in a variety of situations. Educators who focus efforts on learning style but then don't encourage diversity among staff are, of course, defeating their own purposes.

A Topic For Staff Development

As a content topic for staff development, "style" offers tremendous opportunity for professional growth in a number of ways. The concepts of individual style differences have implications for all areas of curriculum and instruction, as illustrated in the circle at the beginning of this section, Figure 12.

We previously discussed how the theories of individual style can be used as a basis for building positive communication and interpersonal relationships. These concepts can become a basis for team-building efforts and for developing skills for peer coaching, for example. Concepts of style can be a basis for encouraging positive communication with parents and with the community at large. They can be a basis for developing effective teacher-student relationships and for encouraging students to interact positively with each other. Ultimately, the climate of a school will depend on the ability of all individuals to respect each other and to value each other's diversity. This respect can come from knowledge about style differences and acceptance of the value of individual patterns of personality.

One school district we work with initially used style to focus on communication and team building among central office staff and building administrators. Then secretaries and support personnel were introduced to basic style concepts and brought together with administrators to strengthen their communication skills and work relationships. "Now I see why you do that!" was a typical comment. Eventually, counselors were included, and school board members and teachers are gradually becoming part of the team focus.

Concepts of style differences can become a basis for *organizing and managing* schools. Studies of individual needs can provide a framework for thinking about organizing the school day, curriculum, class routines and schedule, discipline policies, elective programs, and team teaching. Since consistency in certain policies is necessary in any large organization, respect for individual differences is a key issue.

When one school district changed from a traditional junior high school structure to the integrated-program organization of a middle school, we used concepts of style to help prepare the staff. Teachers examined their own styles in light of their new roles and challenges. They worked with each other in their new teams to plan for making the best use of their individual strengths. They practiced joint curriculum planning and focused on finding ways to accommodate needs of students with diverse styles.

Another content topic for staff development emanating from the study of style is the development of a broad repertoire of *teaching strategies* and teaching behaviors. When teachers understand their own styles and are helped to reflect on the strengths and limitations of those approaches for diverse groups of students, they can identify ways to stretch their own teaching patterns. Individual growth efforts will be more meaningful when they relate directly to the personal needs, goals, and style of each teacher.

Teachers at one school invited a colleague of ours to help them "stretch" their teaching styles. Working with one model of style, they initially developed self-awareness about their teaching styles. They then examined students' learning style needs. Each teacher prepared a personal growth plan identifying goals and actions for trying new teaching behaviors. They worked in subgroups and used peer coaching to implement their plans. A rainbow-colored button reading "We Teach With Style" became a proud symbol of their efforts and commitment.

Underlying the diversity in teaching strategies is, of course, the concept that students are different and need to learn in different ways. Dealing directly with *learning style* is a very important area for staff development. Teachers and administrators need to recognize the different learning styles at work in the classroom. When the intuitive learner asks a tangential question, the teacher should understand how to respond. When the sensing learner asks for a practical example, the teacher should understand that student's need. Teachers need to ask both general and specific questions. They need to provide opportunities for the extraverted student to act while thinking and for the introverted student to think before acting. When teachers give assignments, they should include auditory, visual, and kinesthetic tasks.

One school district formed teams of administrators and teachers from each school to study student learning styles. We worked with them to develop their awareness of different aspects of learning style by introducing several research models. Over the past three years, the individual school teams have applied the concepts in different ways. Some have focused on curriculum materials, some on teaching methods, and others on student-teacher relationships. One group used information on field-dependent-independent perception to expand the teaching of reading beyond a totally phonic approach. One elementary school designed a bookmark for their reading text which lists modality-style characteristics as they apply to reading. The teachers use the bookmark as a daily reminder to direct their reading instruction to all modality strengths.

A variety of other topics lend themselves well to a study of style. In previous chapters we spoke about evaluation, counseling, study skills, higher-level thinking, computers, and parenting. These and many other areas can provide specific topics for staff development.

How to Use Style

Three steps are necessary to design staff development using concepts of style. The first is an awareness and knowledge of the concepts, ideas, and issues. This awareness must be thorough enough that each individual is able to develop a personal understanding of style. This takes time. An introduction to style must be given by someone knowledgeable about style and sincere about celebrating diversity. A person introducing style to others must know the research, understand the complexities and subtleties of the concepts, and be able to model respect for differences.

Once aware of style differences, people must make a personal commitment to respect and honor individual diversity. For many educators this is a reaffirmation of their values and beliefs, while for others it is a new challenge. For all of us it includes a reminder that it is much easier to accept individual diversity in theory than in practice; that it is much easier to say we respect uniqueness than it is to treat all people with that respect!

Once the awareness and personal commitment have been developed, each staff member needs to develop a plan of action and to ask a fundamental question: What effect will the concepts of style have on my professional behavior? It is at this point that staff members should have some options for applying the information about styles. It is a contradiction in terms to espouse a theory of individual style and then require all staff members to apply the theory in exactly the same way. The concepts themselves are obviously better served when staff members individually or as a group develop their own plans for applications. Some people may want to work toward accommodating diversity in curriculum. Others may want to work on their interpersonal relationships and communication with other staff members. Some staff may choose to work on their classroom management and discipline strategies.

This emphasis on individual options does not negate the importance of the staff of a school working toward a common vision and shared goals. Style becomes important as individual staff members decide how to reach the goals. When a school identifies positive climate as a goal, for example, how will each staff member strive to reach it? Or if improved reading skills is the goal, how will each staff member respond? Administrators can hold each staff member accountable for making efforts toward a school goal while still respecting the individual staffer's way of reaching that goal.

Finally, we have learned a lot in the last few years about successful staff development. We know that such efforts must be supported with appropriate follow-up and resources. We know that staff development efforts should involve a commitment from all levels of the professional staff. Here, too, concepts of style should direct an approach to staff development. Those who are planning to use style in staff development efforts must practice what they preach. They must be knowledgeable about styles and also committed to the practice of style.

A Final Word

In many ways the homily of the oyster and the pearl can be used to summarize our attitudes about individual differences in style. Irritations get into the oyster's shell, and the oyster doesn't like them. But when it accepts their reality, it settles down to make one of the most beautiful things in the world—a pearl.

When people are fundamentally different from us, it can cause irritations. But these very differences, when appreciated, can be used to benefit all.

The study of style should be a positive reminder of the reason most of us chose to be educators—the challenge of helping individual students to reach their full potential. The implementation of style is a joyous celebration of diversity!

ANNOTATED BIBLIOGRAPHY

Association for Supervision and Curriculum Development. *Educational Leadership* 36 (January 1979).
Entire issue devoted to learning styles. Articles by Gregorc, the Dunns, and others.

Barbe, Walter B. *Growing Up Learning.* Washington, D.C.: Acropolis Books Ltd., 1985. (Colortone Building, 2400 17th St., N.W., Washington, D.C.)
Written for parents, discusses children's modality strengths and gives suggestions for parents at home and for working with schools.

Barbe, Walter B. and Swassing, Raymond H. *Teaching Through Modality Strengths: Concepts and Practices.* Columbus, OH: Zaner-Bloser, Inc., 1979.
Defines modality, reviews the history of modality-based instruction, describes ways to identify modality strengths, and offers practical suggestions for instruction.

Barth, Roland S. *Run School Run.* Cambridge, Mass.: Harvard University Press, 1980.
A public school principal's story of creating a school that builds upon diversity among students, teachers, and parents. A how-to book that describes organizational decisions that value diversity rather than uniformity.

Becher, Paula; Bledsoe, Larry; and Mok, Paul. *The Strategic Woman.* Dallas, Tex.: Training Associates Press, 1977. (1177 Rockingham, Richardson, TX 75080)
Based on the four personality types described by Carl Jung, this book focuses on personal growth and strategies for interpersonal relationships.

Bolton, Robert, and Bolton, Dorothy Grover. *Social Style/Management Style.* New York: American Management Associations, 1984. (135 West 50th St., New York, NY 10020)
Identifies four social styles based on the work of David Merrill and Roger Reid. Discusses self-awareness and applying style to interpersonal relationships, careers, goal-setting, and management.

Butler, Kathleen A. *It's All in Your Mind: A Student's Guide to Style.* Columbia, Conn.: The Learner's Dimension, 1988. (Box 6, Columbia, CT 06237)

Butler, Kathleen A. *Learning and Teaching Style in Theory and Practice.* Columbia, Conn.: The Learner's Dimension, 1984, revised 1987. (Box 6, Columbia, CT 06237)
Based on Gregorc's style model, this book presents the concept of style with ex-

tensive examples in learning and teaching. It offers practical, detailed suggestions for utilizing style in instruction and curriculum.

Carbo, Marie; Dunn, Rita; and Dunn, Kenneth. *Teaching Students to Read Through Their Individual Learning Styles.* Englewood Cliffs, N.J.: Prentice Hall, 1986.
  Describes Dunn and Dunn's model of styles and Carbo's application to reading, with extensive examples of adapting reading materials to meet students' learning styles.

Claxton, Charles S., and Ralston, Yvonne. *Learning Styles: Their Impact on Teaching and Administration.* Washington, D.C.: American Association for Higher Education, 1978.
  The first part gives a good overview of the research on cognitive styles. Written for application at the college level.

Cornett, Claudia E. *What You Should Know About Teaching and Learning Styles.* Bloomington, Ind.: Phi Delta Kappa Educational Foundation, 1983.
  An overview of learning styles, drawing the relationship to teaching styles and brain research. Includes a detailed list of assessment instruments and suggestions for accommodating learning styles.

Dunn, Rita and Dunn, Kenneth. *Teaching Students Through Their Individual Learning Styles: A Practical Approach.* Reston, Va.: Reston Publishing Co., Inc., 1978.
  Describes detailed classroom activities and lessons that respond to various student learning styles as defined by the Dunns' 18 elements.

Entwistle, Noel. *Styles of Learning and Teaching.* New York: John Wiley & Sons, 1981.
  An integrated outline of important aspects of educational psychology focusing on the processes of learning and teaching and how people differ in their approaches.

Gardner, Howard. *Frames of Mind: The Theory of Multiple Intelligences.* New York: Basic Books, 1983.
  Identifies and describes Multiple Intelligences, including Musical Intelligence, Spatial Intelligence, Bodily-Kinesthetic Intelligence, and Personal Intelligence.

Garger, Stephen. "Learning Styles: A State of the Art and a Curriculum Design for Application." Doctoral dissertation, Seattle University, 1982. (Available from University Microfilms International, Ann Arbor, Michigan.)
  A review of the literature on styles and a description of a curriculum project implementing styles in the counseling department at a high school.

Golay, Keith. *Learning Patterns and Temperament Styles.* Newport Beach, Calif.: Manas-Systems, 1982. (P.O. Box 106, Newport Beach, CA 92663)
  Based on Keirsey's work with Jung's theories and Myers-Briggs definitions, this book profiles four types of learners and offers specific suggestions for accommodating the styles through the physical environment, tasks, subject interests, and classroom climate.

Goldstein, Kenneth, and Blackman, Sheldon. *Cognitive Style, Five Approaches and Relevant Research.* New York: John Wiley & Sons, 1978.

Addressed to behavioral scientists, this book reviews various approaches to the study of cognitive style. It cites extensive research and theories.

Gregorc, Anthony F. *An Adult's Guide to Style.* Maynard, Mass.: Gabriel Systems, Inc., 1982. (P.O. Box 357, Maynard, MA 01754)
An overview of Gregorc's style work with an emphasis on self-awareness, acceptance of others' styles, and development of abilities to stretch and flex one's style.

Gregorc, Anthony F. *Inside Styles: Beyond the Basics.* Maynard, Mass.: Gabriel Systems, Inc., 1987. (P.O. Box 357, Maynard, MA 01754)
Gregorc responds to questions about his research, expanding and enlarging his view of style and its meaning for student and teacher, therapist and patient, administrator and faculty, supervisor and employee.

Guild, Patricia O'Rourke Burke. "Learning Styles: Knowledge, Issues and Applications for Classroom Teachers." Doctoral dissertation, University of Massachusetts, 1980. (Available from University Microfilms International, Ann Arbor, Michigan, #80-19,462.)
An overview of the literature on learning styles leading to generalizations for teachers and some suggested directions for classroom accommodation.

Guild, Pat, and Hand, Kathi. *Where Did We Get This One? A Parents' Guide to Appreciating the Individual Personalities of Their Children.* Seattle: The Teaching Advisory, 1985. (Box 99131, Seattle WA 98199)
A booklet designed to help parents understand differences in style and use this knowledge to enhance their children's self-esteem, improve parent-child relationships, and help children have more success in school.

Harrison, Allen F., and Bramson, Robert M. *Styles of Thinking, Strategies for Asking Questions, Making Decisions, and Solving Problems.* Garden City, N.Y.: Anchor Press/Doubleday, 1982.
Addressed to a business audience, this book describes five Styles of Thinking originally identified by C. West Churchman and Ian Mitroff. It discusses ways to use strengths and to extend personal-thinking strategies.

Jung, C.G. *Psychological Types.* Princeton, N.J.: Princeton University Press, 1971 (orig. pub. 1921).
Thorough description of Jung's theory of psychological types.

Keefe, James W. *Learning Style Theory and Practice.* Reston, Va.: National Association of Secondary School Principals, 1987.
A summary of Keefe's review of cognitive, affective, and physiological models of learning styles, with information on brain behavior and application.

Keirsey, David, and Bates, Marilyn. *Please Understand Me, Character and Temperament Types.* Del Mar, Calif.: Prometheus, Nemesis, 1978. (P.O. Box 2082, Del Mar, CA 92014)
Based on the 16 Myers-Briggs types, this book proposes four temperament types and offers general examples of type in everyday life, as well as in teaching and learning.

Kirby, Patricia. *Cognitive Style, Learning Style and Transfer Skill Acquisition.* Columbus: The National Center for Research in Vocational Education, The Ohio State University, 1979. (1960 Kenny Road, Columbus, OH 43210)

Links cognitive and learning style research and theory to the world of work, focusing on the understanding of and ability to use transfer skills and cognitive/learning styles.

Lawrence, Gordon. *People Types and Tiger Stripes, A Practical Guide to Learning Styles.* Gainesville, Fla.: Center for Applications of Psychological Type, Inc., 1982. (2720 N.W. Sixth St., Gainesville, FL 32601)

Based on the Myers-Briggs descriptions of 16 types, this book gives an overview of style and some practical suggestions for instruction, meeting students' developmental needs, considering teaching styles, and organizing staff development programs on styles.

Littauer, Florence. *Personality Plus.* Old Tappan, N.J.: Fleming H. Revell Company, 1983.

Utilizing the terms Sanguine, Choleric, Melancholy, and Phlegmatic established by Hippocrates, this book emphasizes building on one's own God-given strengths and improving relations with others.

Mamchur, Carolyn Marie. *Insights, Understanding Yourself and Others.* Toronto, Ontario: The Ontario Institute for Studies in Education, 1984. (252 Bloor St. West, Toronto, Ontario M5S 1V6)

An exploration of the world of psychological types, based on Carl Jung's concepts. Uses stories, photographs, paintings, and dramatic vignettes to discuss the full potential of the human spirit.

May, Rollo; Angel, Ernest; and Ellenberger, Henri F., eds. *Existence. A New Dimension in Psychiatry and Psychology.* New York: Simon and Schuster, 1958.

A good, readable explanation of existentialism and the existential approach to therapy.

McCarthy, Bernice. *The 4MAT System: Teaching to Learning Styles with Right/Left Mode Techniques.* Barrington, Ill.: Excel, Inc., 1980. (Box 706, Barrington, IL 60010)

A model for teaching based on Kolb's experiential-learning cycle. Includes a variety of sample lessons.

Merrill, David, and Reid, Roger. *Personal Styles and Effective Performance.* Radnor, Pa.: Chilton Book Company, 1981.

Approached from the perspective observing of social behavior, this book describes styles with extensive examples from business. A good section on versatility.

Myers, Isabel Briggs. *Introduction to Type.* Palo Alto, Calif.: Consulting Psychologists Press, Inc., 1962. (577 College Ave., Palo Alto, CA 94306)

A comprehensive booklet describing the Myers-Briggs types and Jung's original type work.

Myers, Isabel Briggs. *Gifts Differing.* Palo Alto, Calif.: Consulting Psychologists Press, Inc., 1980. (577 College Ave., Palo Alto, CA 94306)

An overview of the Myers-Briggs descriptions of 16 types based on Carl Jung's work on psychological types. Emphasis on the effect of type on personality and human development. Brief section on learning styles.

National Association of Secondary School Principals, eds. *Student Learning Styles: Diagnosing and Prescribing Programs.* Reston, Va.: National Association of Secondary School Principals, 1979. (1904 Association Dr., Reston, VA 22091)

A collection of articles on learning styles by several major researchers in the field. General Editor James W. Keefe presents an overview in the opening chapter.

National Association of Secondary School Principals, eds. *Student Learning Styles and Brain Behavior: Programs, Instrumentation, Research.* Reston, Va.: National Association of Secondary School Principals, 1982. (1904 Association Dr., Reston, VA 22091)

A collection of articles from a major NASSP conference on learning styles and brain research. Focuses on programs, research, instrumentation and applications.

Samples, Bob; Hammond, Bill; and McCarthy, Bernice. *4MAT and Science: Toward Wholeness in Science Education.* Barrington Ill.: EXCEL, Inc., 1980 (Box 706, Barrington, IL 60010)

Demonstrates how 4MAT applies to the teaching of science, addresses recent trends in science education, and includes lesson plans.

Sheive, Linda T., and Schoenheit, Marian B. *Leadership: Examining the Elusive.* Alexandria, Va.: Association for Supervision and Curriculum Development, 1987 (yearbook).

Includes references to diversity of styles among educational leaders and a chapter on leadership styles by Pat Guild.

Silver, Harvey F., and Hanson, J. Robert. *Teaching Styles and Strategies.* Morristown, N.J.: Banson Silver and Strong Associates, Inc., 1982. (Box 402, Morristown, NJ 08057).

Describes the Hanson-Silver model of learning styles, based on Jung's theory, and matches standard teaching strategies to learning styles.

Simon, Anita, and Byram, Claudia. *You've Got to Reach 'Em to Teach 'Em.* Dallas, Tex.: Training Associates Press, 1977. (1177 Rockingham, Richardson, TX 75080)

Based on four communicating styles identified by Carl Jung and described by Paul Mok, this book gives an overview of styles and their implications for teaching and learning. It offers many practical suggestions for teachers, especially for style-flexing.

Tyler, Leona E. *The Psychology of Human Differences.* 3rd ed. New York: Appleton-Century-Crofts, 1965.

A comprehensive text on individual differences describing some factors that produce these differences.

Ulrich, Cindy, and Guild, Pat. *No Sweat! How To Use Your Learning Style To Be A Better Student.* Seattle: The Teaching Advisory, 1985. (Box 99131, Seattle, WA 98199)

A booklet written for students to help them identify their own best ways of learning and use their learning style effectively in school. Includes suggestions for studying effectively, ways to approach particular assignments and for getting help from teachers and parents.

Wickes, Frances G. *The Inner World of Childhood.* Englewood Cliffs, N.J.: Prentice-Hall, Inc., 1966 (orig. pub. 1927).

A sensitive exploration of the intricacies within a parent-child relationship by a Jungian-trained child psychologist. One chapter focuses directly on psychological types.

Witkin, Herman, and Goodenough, Donald R. *Cognitive Styles: Essence and Origins.* New York: International Universities Press, Inc., 1981. (Available from Consulting Psychologists Press, Inc., 577 College Ave., Palo Alto, CA 94306)

Covers the historical development of field-dependence-independence and psychological differentiation and the origins of cognitive styles. Summarizes and cites extensive research.

REFERENCES

Allport, Gordon W. *Pattern and Growth in Personality.* New York: Holt, Rinehart and Winston, 1937, 1961.

Barbe, Walter B., and Milone, Michael N. "What We Know About Modality Strengths." *Educational Leadership* 38, 5 (February 1981): 378-380.

Barbe, Walter B., and Milone, Michael N. "Teaching Through Modality Strengths: Look Before You Leap." In *Student Learning Styles and Brain Behavior,* pp. 54-57. Reston, Va: National Association of Secondary School Principals, 1982.

Barbe, Walter B., and Swassing, Raymond H. *Teaching Through Modality Strengths: Concepts and Practices.* Columbus, Ohio: Zaner-Bloser, Inc., 1979. (P.O. Box 16764, Columbus OH 43216)

Barbe W.; Swassing, R; and Milone, M. *The Swassing-Barbe Modality Index in the Zaner-Bloser Modality Kit.* Columbus, Ohio: Zaner- Bloser, Inc., 1979. (P.O. Box 16764, Columbus OH 43216)

Barth, Roland S. *Run School Run.* Cambridge, Mass.: Harvard University Press, 1980.

Butler, Kathleen A. *Learning and Teaching Style In Theory and Practice.* Maynard, Mass.: Gabriel Systems, Inc., 1984.

Cantor, Nathaniel. *Dynamics of Learning.* New York: Agathon Press, Inc., 1946/1972 (distributed by Schocken Books, Inc., NY).

Carbo, Marie. "Reading Style Inventory." Roslyn Heights, N.Y.: Learning Research Associates, 1981. (P.O. Box 39, Roslyn Heights, NY 11577)

Carbo, Marie. "Teaching Reading the Way Children Learn to Read." Early Years (February 1982): 43-46.

Coates, Susan. *Preschool Embedded Figures Test.* Palo Alto, Calif.: Consulting Psychologists Press, Inc., 1972.

Combs, Arthur W.; Avila, Donald L.; and Purkey, William. *Helping Relationships, Basic Concepts for the Helping Professions.* Boston: Allyn and Bacon, Inc., 1971.

Cornett, Claudia E. *What You Should Know About Teaching and Learning Styles.* Bloomington, Ind.: Phi Delta Kappa Educational Foundation, 1983.

Dunn, Rita. "Teaching Students Through Their Individual Learning Styles: A Research Report." In *Student Learning Styles and Brain Behavior.* Reston, Va.: National Association of Secondary School Principals, 1982, pp. 142-151.

Dunn, Rita, and Dunn, Kenneth. *Educator's Self-Teaching Guide to Individualizing Instructional Programs.* New York: Parker Publishing Company, 1975a.

Dunn, Rita, and Dunn, Kenneth. "Finding the Best Fit: Learning Styles, Teaching Styles." *NASSP Bulletin* 59 (October 1975b): 37-49.

Dunn, Rita; Dunn, Kenneth; and Price, Gary E. "Learning Style Inventory" and "Productivity Environmental Preference Survey." Lawrence, Kans.: Price Systems, Inc., 1975, 1978 (LSI), 1979 (PEPS). (Box 3067, Lawrence, KS 66046)

Foshay, Arthur W. "Curriculum Talk." In *Considered Action for Curriculum Improvement.* Alexandria, Va.: Association for Supervision and Curriculum Development, 1980, pp. 82-94.

Gardner, Howard. *Frames of Mind: The Theory of Multiple Intelligences.* New York: Basic Books, 1983.

Garger, Stephen, and Guild, Pat. "Learning Styles: The Crucial Differences." *Curriculum Review* 23 1 (February 1984): 9- 12.

Garger, Stephen, and Guild, Pat. "Schooling: Getting In Style With Our Times." *Context and Conflict,* Journal of the Washington State Association for Supervision and Curriculum Development, 13, 1 (Spring/Summer, 1985): 11-12.

Glatthorn, Allan A. *Differentiated Supervision.* Alexandria, Va.: Association for Supervision and Curriculum Development, 1984.

Golay, Keith. *Learning Patterns and Temperament Styles.* Newport Beach, Calif.: Manas-Systems, 1982.

Goodlad, John I. *A Place Called School, Prospects for the Future.* New York: McGraw-Hill Book Company, 1984.

Gregorc, Anthony F. *An Adult's Guide to Style.* Maynard, Mass.: Gabriel Systems, Inc., 1982. (P.O. Box 357, Maynard, MA 01754)

Gregorc, Anthony. *Gregorc Style Delineator.* Maynard, Mass.: Gabriel Systems, Inc., 1978, 1982. (P.O. Box 357, Maynard, MA 01754)

Guild, Patricia O'Rourke Burke. *"Learning Styles: Knowledge, Issues and Applications for Classroom Teachers."* Ed.D dissertation, University of Massachusetts, 1980.

Guild, Pat. "Learning Styles: Understanding Before Action." *Context and Conflict* (Journal of the Washington State Association for Supervision and Curriculum Development) 10 (Summer 1982): 4-6.

Guild, Pat. "Different Gifts in Learning." *Parish Teacher* 7, 10 (June 1984): 6.

Guild, Pat., and Hand, Kathi. *Where Did We Get This One? A Parents' Guide to Appreciating the Individual Personalities of Their Children.* Seattle: The Teaching Advisory, 1985. (P.O. Box 99131, Seattle, WA 98199)

Hoffman, Jeffrey L., and Betkouski, Marianne. "A Summary of Myers-Briggs Type Indicator Research Applications in Education." In *Research in Psychological Type* 3. Edited by Thomas G. Carskadon, MS: Mississippi State University, 1981, pp. 3-41.

Hunter, Madeline. "Diagnostic Teaching." *The Elementary School Journal* 80, (September 1979): 41-46.

James, William. *The Principles of Psychology, Vol. 1.* Boston: Harvard University Press, 1890, 1981.

Joyce, Bruce R.; Hersh, Richard H.; and McKibbin, Michael. *The Structure of School Improvement.* New York: Longman, 1983.

Jung, C.G. *Psychological Types.* Princeton, N.J.: Princeton University Press, 1971 (orig. pub. 1921).

Kagan, Jerome. "Reflection-Impulsivity: The Generality and Dynamics of Conceptual Tempo." *Journal of Abnormal Psychology* 71 1, (1966): 17-24.

Karp, Stephen A. and Konstadt, Norma. *Children's Embedded Figures Test.* Palo Alto, Calif.: Consulting Psychologists Press, Inc., 1971.

Keefe, James W. "Foreword." In *Student Learning Styles and Brain Behavior: Programs, Instrumentation, Research.* Reston, Va.: National Association of Secondary School Principals, 1982.

Keirsey, David, and Bates, Marilyn. *Please Understand Me, Character and Temperament Types.* Del Mar, Calif.: Prometheus, Nemesis, 1978.

Klein, George S. "The Personal World Through Perception." In *Perception, An Approach to Personality,* pp. 328-355. Edited by Robert R. Blake and Glenn V. Ramsey. New York: Ronald Press, 1951.

Kolb, David. *Learning Style Inventory.* Boston: McBer and Company, 1976. (137 Newberry St., Boston, MA 02116)

Kuhn, Thomas S. *The Structure of Scientific Revolutions.* Chicago: University of Chicago Press, 1961, 1970.

Kusler, Gerald E. "Getting To Know You." In *Student Learning Styles and Brain Behavior: Programs, Instumentation, Research,* pp. 11- 14. Reston, Va.: National Association of Secondary School Principals, 1982.

Lawrence, Gordon. *People Types and Tiger Stripes, A Practical Guide to Learning Styles.* Gainesville, Fla.: Center for Applications of Psychological Type, Inc., 1982.

Learning Styles Network, School of Education and Human Services, St. John's University, Grand Central and Utopia Parkways, Jamaica, NY 11439.

Letteri, Charles A. "Cognitive Profile: Basic Determinant of Academic Achievement." *The Journal of Educational Research* 73, 4 (March/April 1980): 195-198.

Lowenfeld, Viktor. "Tests for Visual and Haptical Aptitudes." The *American Journal of Psychology* 58, 1 (January 1945): 100-111.

May, Rollo, ed. *Existential Psychology.* New York: Random House, 1961, 1969.

Angel, Ernest, and Ellenberger, Henri F., eds. *Existence. A New Dimension in Psychiatry and Psychology.* New York: Simon and Schuster, 1958.

McCarthy, Bernice. *The 4MAT System: Teaching to Learning Styles with Right/Left Mode Techniques.* Barrington, Ill.: EXCEL, Inc., 1980.

McCarthy, Bernice. "What 4MAT Training Teaches Us About Staff Development." *Educational Leadership* 42, 7 (April 1985): 61-68.

McCarthy, Bernice, and Lafler, Susan, eds. *4MAT In Action: Creative Lesson Plans for Teaching To Learning Styles With Right/Left Mode Techniques.* Barrington, Ill.: EXCEL, 1983.

McCaulley, Mary. H., and Natter, Frank L. *Psychological (Myers- Briggs) Type Differences in Education.* Gainesville, Fla.: Center For Applications of Psychological Type, Inc., 1974, 1980.

Mackenzie, Donald E. "Research for School Improvement: An Appraisal of Some Recent Trends." *Educational Researcher* (April 1983): 5-17.

Milone, Michael N., Jr. "Modality and the Kindergarten Child." In *Zaner-Bloser Kindergarten Resource Book,* p. xiii. Columbus: Zaner-Bloser, Inc., 1980.

Mok, Paul P. "Communicating Styles Survey." Dallas, Tex.: Training Associates Press, 1975. (1177 Rockingham, Richardson, TX 75080)

Myers, Isabel Briggs. *Introduction to Type.* Palo Alto, Calif.: Consulting Psychologists Press, Inc., 1962.

Myers, Isabel Briggs, and Briggs, Katharine C. "Myers-Briggs Type Indicator." Palo Alto, Calif.: Consulting Psychologists Press, Inc., 1943, 1976. (577 College Ave., Palo Alto, CA 94306)

Oltman, Philip K.; Raskin, Evelyn; and Witkin, Herman A. *Group Embedded Figures Test.* Palo Alto, Calif.: Consulting Psychologists Press, Inc., 1971.

Peters, Thomas J., and Waterman, Robert Jr. *In Search of Excellence.* New York: Harper & Row, 1982.

Ramirez, M., and Castaneda, A. *Cultural Democracy, Bicognitive Development and Education.* New York: Academic Press, 1974.

Restak, Richard M. *The Brain: The Last Frontier.* New York: Doubleday and Company, 1979.

Rutter, Michael; Maughan, Barbara; Motimore, Peter; and Ouston, Janet; with Smith, Alan. *Fifteen Thousand Hours, Secondary Schools and Their Effects on Children.* Cambridge, Mass.: Harvard University Press, 1979.

Samples, Bob; Hammond, Bill, and McCarthy; Bernice. *4MAT and Science: Toward Wholeness in Science Education.* Barrington, Ill.: EXCEL, 1985.

Simon, Anita, and Byram, Claudia. *You've Got to Reach 'Em to Teach 'Em.* Dallas, Tex.: Training Associates Press, 1977.

Sizer, Theodore R. *Horace's Compromise, The Dilemma of the American High School.* Boston: Houghton Mifflin Company, 1984.

Toffler, Alvin. *The Third Wave.* New York: Bantam Books, 1981.

Tyler, Leona E. *The Psychology of Human Differences.* 3rd ed. New York: Appleton-Century-Crofts, 1965.

Ulrich, Cindy, and Guild, Pat. *No Sweat! How To Use Your Learning Style To Be A Better Student.* Seattle: The Teaching Advisory, 1985. (P.O. Box 99131, Seattle, WA 98199)

Walker, Decker F. "A Barnstorming Tour of Writing on Curriculum." In *Considered Action for Curriculum Improvement.* Alexandria, Va.: Association for Supervision and Curriculum Development, 1980, pp. 71-81.

Wickes, Frances G. *The Inner World of Childhood.* Englewood Cliffs, N.J.: Prentice-Hall, Inc., 1966 (orig. pub. 1927).

Witkin, Herman A. "Embedded Figures Test." Palo Alto, Calif.: Consulting Psychologists Press, Inc., 1969. (577 College Ave., Palo Alto, CA 94306)

Witkin, Herman A.; Moore, C. A.; Goodenough, D. R.; and Cox, P. W. "Field-Dependent and Field-Independent Cognitive Styles and Their Educational Implications." *Review of Educational Research* 47 (Winter 1977): 1-64.

Witkin, Herman A.; Oldman, P. K.; Cox, Pat W.; Ehrlichman, Elizabeth; Hamm, Robert M.; and Ringler, Robert W. *Field-Dependence-Independence and Psychological Differentiation, A Bibliography.* Princeton, N.J.: Educational Testing Service, 1973 (Supplements 1-5, 1974-1981; also available from Consulting Psychologists Press, Inc., Palo Alto, CA).

Yalom, Irvin D. *Existential Psychotherapy.* New York: Basic Books, 1980.

ABOUT THE AUTHORS

Pat Guild is president of Pat Guild Associates (Seattle, Wash.), an organization that trains administrators, teachers, parents, and people in business and other professions to use personal diversity productively in communication, team building, management, teaching, and learning. She is coordinator of Learning Style Programs and serves on the graduate faculty at Seattle Pacific University, and has taught at the University of Washington and Seattle University. She has worked in teacher education and staff development for 15 years, was an elementary school principal in Massachusetts and a teacher in New York City and Connecticut. She earned her doctorate in International Education and Teacher Education at the University of Massachusetts in 1980; her dissertation is entitled "Learning Styles: Knowledge, Issues and Applications for Classroom Teachers."

Stephen Garger has been a teacher, counselor, and administrator in high schools in New York City; Missoula, Montana; and Seattle, Washington. He has implemented learning styles as a school counselor and in his private practice. He has conducted numerous seminars for teachers and parents and taught courses as adjunct faculty at Seattle University, Seattle Pacific University, and at St. Martin's College (Lacy, Wash.). He is director of the Issaquah (Wash.) School District's Alternative School. He earned his doctorate in Educational Leadership at Seattle University in 1982; his dissertation is entitled "Learning Styles: A State of the Art and a Curriculum Design for Application."